Diversity in the Workplace

Diversity in the Workplace

Eye-Opening Interviews
to Jumpstart Conversations about
Identity, Privilege, and Bias

Bärí A. Williams, Esq.

**ROCKRIDGE
PRESS**

Interior and Cover Designer: Erin Yeung
Art Producer: Karen Williams
Editor: Crystal Nero
Production Manager: Riley Hoffman
Production Editor: Melissa Edeburn

Illustrations © Lavender Design Co/Creative Market cover and pp. ii, v, vi, xvii, xviii, 20, 38, 58, and 76.

Author photo courtesy of © Jean de Paul Eustache.

ISBN: Print 978-1-64152-904-4 | Ebook 978-1-64152-905-1

R0

The interviews in this book have been edited for length and clarity.

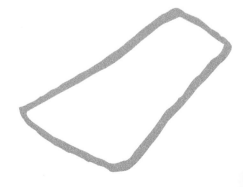

*To my grandmother, Bettye; my mom, Linda;
and Jaime, Gabriel, and Adrienne. I do what
I do for, and because of, them and our people.*

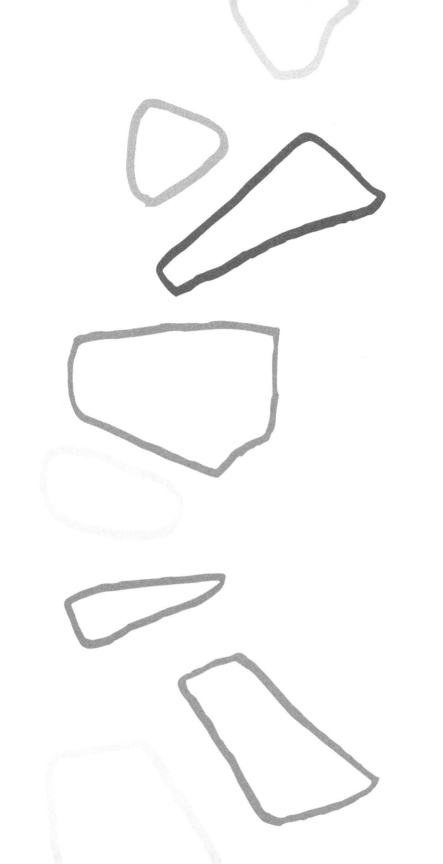

Contents

Introduction

Where We Are Today

The history of work in the United States has always been fraught with inequities. The many advancements that have been made are largely the result of the labor movement's hard-fought struggle for workers' rights. Unfortunately, these rights have often been applied unequally.

Addressing internal and external issues of inequity demonstrates to employees that companies care about them holistically, which fosters a sense of belonging. To create an inclusive workplace, it is essential for company leaders to understand the history of employee rights and the myriad experiences that employees bring, and cope with, in the workplace. Diversity may get people in the door; inclusion keeps them there. Let's dive in.

How Do We Define Diversity?

Diversity refers to the distinct traits that make a person unique, such as sex, race, gender, religion, education, age, ability, and national origin and culture. This book touches on two types of diversity: identity and cognitive.

Identity diversity (also called representational diversity) is reflected in the immutable characteristics that define an individual's lived experiences, such as being differently abled or being a person of color.

These differences directly influence a person's day-to-day encounters, access, and opportunities.

Cognitive diversity refers to the different ways that people think, problem-solve, and express themselves. A cognitively diverse workplace may comprise introverts, extroverts, and those who have different communication styles. Cognitive diversity can be heavily influenced by identity diversity through the experiences of people with different racial and ethnic backgrounds, abilities, religions, genders, and sexual identities.

Both identity and cognitive diversity make a person unique, and it is the interaction among unique people that makes an organization diverse. This book will explore the experiences of people from a variety of backgrounds to help readers understand how individuals' experiences influence, not just company and team output, but individual output as well. Company success depends on individual success, which is inextricably tied to an employee's experience.

A Cultural Snapshot

Workplace discrimination can come in various forms, such as not hiring or promoting someone because of that person's religious garb or denying a woman a work assignment because she's pregnant. It could also manifest as withdrawing an opportunity from a differently abled person or making jokes about someone's age.

For employees who come from marginalized communities, the pressure to survive—and thrive—within workplace hierarchies can be incredibly stressful. In prior decades, discussions about race, religion, ethnicity, culture, and politics were typically avoided in professional environments. In today's workplaces, such discussions are much more common. Many crucial conversations about diversity in the workplace are informed by current events, and controversial political and social stances are having an increasingly greater impact in the office.

In fact, the workforce is beginning to embrace social justice and activism. CEOs of several major companies have taken a stance on issues from racism to police shootings, and some have introduced new policies reflecting changing societal mores. In March 2019, the CEOs of Wells Fargo and JPMorgan Chase chose to divest from private prisons. In June 2019, Bank of America announced that it would no longer finance the operations of prisons and detention centers.

In the wake of the #MeToo movement, which exploded on social media in fall 2017, several companies introduced new policies to protect employees from sexual misconduct. For example, Condé Nast International, publisher of *Vogue*, *GQ*, and *Teen Vogue* magazines, adopted new rules that prohibit hiring models under 18 years of age and require private dressing rooms for models during photo shoots.

How Did We Get Here? A Brief History of Employee Rights

Workers' rights have been a flash point for America since its beginnings. Although there have been significant gains, there are mountains still left to climb. Let's look at key moments in the past 100 years in the fight for workplace equality and protection.

At the end of the Civil War in 1865, work moved from farms to factories, and higher wages spread from the North to the South. With the passage of the 13th Amendment abolishing slavery and the 14th Amendment granting citizenship to all those born or naturalized in the United States, the right to paid labor was seemingly available to all. However, restrictive laws known as "black codes" were implemented that limited the types of work black people could do in addition to when, where, and how they could do it.

Women's rights were addressed with the passage of the Equal Pay Act of 1963, which amended the Fair Labor Standards Act of 1938 to ensure that men and women received equal pay for equal work. That mandate still has not been fully realized. The Lilly Ledbetter Fair Pay Act of 2009 stipulated that women could sue for pay disparity. This act was later nullified by President Donald Trump, who also announced the cessation of an Obama-era rule requiring businesses with more than 100 employees to collect wage data by demographics (gender, race, and ethnicity). President Trump's move means disparities are harder to track, and thus discrimination is more difficult to prove.

The Civil Rights Act of 1964 sought to level the employment playing field by banning employment discrimination based on "race, color, religion, sex, or national origin." The act also created the Equal Employment Opportunity Commission, which oversees federal enforcement of antidiscrimination laws in employment, in addition to prohibiting the use of federal funds for any discriminatory program.

Equal protection for those with different abilities was realized with the passage of the Americans with Disabilities Act of 1990, prohibiting discrimination against individuals with disabilities and ensuring they have equal access, rights, and opportunities. It also requires that employers provide reasonable accommodations—for example, work-from-home days for those with constant pain or limited movement, or modified work rooms and lighting for those with sight issues—if there is no undue financial burden.

The final frontier in the fight for workers' rights is equal protection under the law for LGBTQ+ citizens. In May 2019, the Equality Act was passed. It amended the Civil Rights Act of 1964 to extend civil rights protections to LGBTQ+ employees. Many states now have laws to prohibit discriminatory hiring and firing practices based on gender identity and sexual orientation.

How to Use This Book

Who Can Benefit from This Book?

Think of this book as a guided tour of what it means to be a minority in the workplace. Although executives can undoubtedly benefit from this book, it is geared toward business professionals at all levels. Ultimately, it's middle managers and peers who have the greatest day-to-day impact on the workplace environment.

If you picked up this book because you are a member of a marginalized community, the interviews presented here can help affirm your experiences in the workplace. It's my hope that the stories detailed in these pages will provide support and validation to those who may feel isolated in their experiences.

Additionally, this book is meant to serve as a resource to inspire and facilitate crucial conversations among managers, employees, and executive teams.

What This Book Is Not

This book provides a snapshot of some workplace experiences born out of socialization, expectation, and learned behaviors that often result in inequitable treatment. Although the book can provide context for how to deal with certain behaviors, it's not a substitute for actual human resources (HR) policy or state and federal law.

Keep in mind that the experiences captured here are in no way reflective of the entire workplace experience of any individual or group. This book is a starting point for examining issues that relate to diversity in order to increase awareness of bias. The interviews collected here are meant to inspire introspection and self-reflection that will lead to positive change.

Life Is Intersectional

Although this book is divided into five categories of identity, the majority of interviewees claim multiple categories. This book recognizes and celebrates the different ways in which the interviewees choose to self-identify. It also acknowledges that some identities may take precedence over others or that they can all be simultaneously influential.

Many companies have embraced the adage "Bring your whole self to work" to demonstrate that they encourage inclusivity for all employees. Being authentic at work means embracing all aspects of yourself. It means feeling free to engage in cultural expression, personal style of dress, and a communication style that works for you—and having the ability to contribute in a meaningful way.

Environment Matters

Be considerate in how you discuss these topics with colleagues. Approach such conversations with a spirit of curiosity, empathy, and understanding. Recognize them as a learning opportunity with something for everyone to gain. Consider who is present and what potential triggers might arise so you can provide a safe space for exchanges of ideas.

Emotional Triggers

Candid conversations require participants to acknowledge that discussions about diversity are likely to elicit strong emotions. Recognize the vulnerability of minorities as well as the discomfort that people in positions of power might feel. Make space for everyone to process and feel the emotions that these conversations may spur.

It's also important to understand the difference between feeling comfortable and feeling safe. Use language that is appropriate to emphasize the idea that exploring uncomfortable realities is a necessary element of change. Be cognizant that not everyone has the appropriate language to describe what they are feeling or observing. Creating a space for these conversations also means recognizing that some colleagues may not have the right vernacular but are willing to learn.

KEY TERMS

ALLY: An individual who contributes time, attention, and/or financial support to a minority organization to amplify and support the agenda of minority voices seeking equity.

CISGENDER (CIS): A term for a person who identifies as the gender that corresponds to the sex assigned to them at birth. *Cis* is the opposite of *trans*.

C-SUITE: An informal term used to describe the most senior executives and directors in a company, that is, CEO, COO, and CFO.

DIVERSITY, EQUITY, INCLUSION, and **BELONGING:** In the workplace context, *diversity* refers to the number of people who represent various demographics; *equity* determines if people are treated equally, including pay rates, once inside the organization; *inclusion* means how they are integrated into the organization and involved in decision making; and *belonging* ensures that people are comfortable and will stay.

IMPOSTER SYNDROME: When an individual doubts their accomplishments and doesn't believe their success is earned. They fear that they will be "found out" or exposed as a fake.

IN-GROUP: A group of people who have a shared identity or interest.

INTERSECTIONALITY: A term coined by professor Kimberlé Crenshaw that initially addressed the challenges of black feminism and has now come to embrace the points of intersection among gender identity, race and ethnicity, socioeconomic identity, familial status, and other types of identity.

MODEL MINORITY: A shorthand term for classifying Asian Americans as smart, dutiful, docile, and intellectually ambitious.

PASSING: Typically an in-group term used to describe how someone in the group may be mistakenly identified as a member of a dominant group. For example, a nonwhite person who looks phenotypically white may be said to "pass" for white.

PRIVILEGE: A special right, advantage, or immunity granted or available only to a particular person or group.

RESPECTABILITY POLITICS: What members of a minority group engage in when they police themselves on the basis of the majority group's values. Instead of embracing their own differences, they attempt to conform under a misguided belief that doing so will protect them.

TRANSGENDER (TRANS): A term referring to people who identify as a gender different from their assigned sex at birth or as any/no gender.

UNCONSCIOUS BIAS: Stereotypes, based on irrational beliefs, that are not obvious to us. These stereotypes aren't always negative; a "halo effect" of unconscious bias inclines us to view our own gender or race more favorably than others.

WHITE SAVIOR: A white person who comes to rescue marginalized people from themselves, their neighborhoods, or their predicaments. White saviors believe that they can overcome structural or institutional racism or discrimination because they are greater than those impediments.

Rules of Engagement

To create a safe space for candid conversations, set these ground rules:

Check your biases at the door. Give some thought to what preconceived notions you may have had about colleagues, and think about why you made those assumptions.

Don't take—or give—negative feedback as a personal attack. Feedback is a tool to make us better, not an unchecked opportunity to criticize coworkers. When used properly, it can provide vital information that leads to improvement.

Allow people to sit with their discomfort. These discussions are about growth and clarification, so don't rush to get past the uncomfortable part. It's perfectly okay to let someone feel what they feel until they reach a point of revelation or insight.

Engage the resistance. Don't be afraid to ask why or try to discern the reasons someone feels the way they do. Approach discussions with respect and intellectual curiosity, not judgment.

Meet people where they are. Approach people from a place of genuine interest and desire for growth. Don't try to diminish the lessons a person has learned from their lived experience.

Identify common beliefs. There are always shared understandings if you look for them.

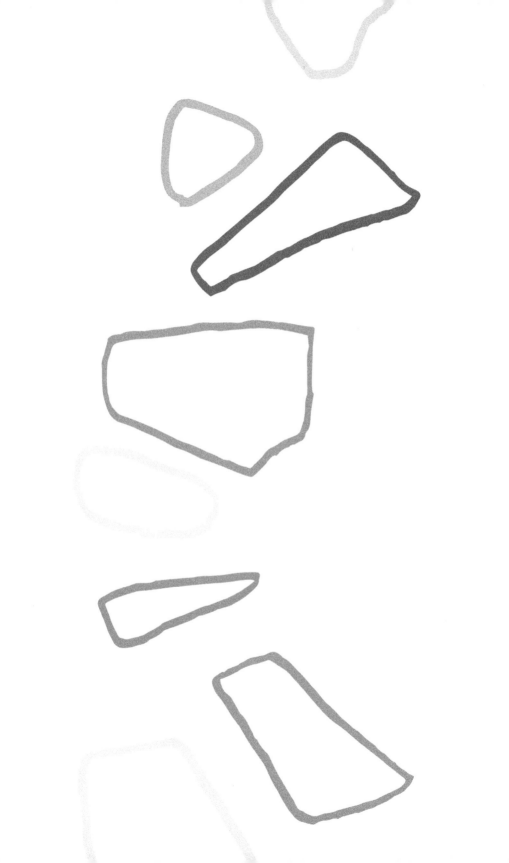

PART ONE

RACE: AMERICA'S ORIGINAL SIN IN THE WORKPLACE

Racialized jobs have deep roots in American history, from the institution of slavery and Chinese immigrants building the transcontinental railroads to Latinx migrants working on produce farms in the present day. Bias has played a role in dictating who can enter certain professions, and many minority groups have been relegated to low-paying, manual-labor jobs for generations. This practice continues today and perpetuates an assumption that nonwhites are unsuited to managerial roles and positions of power.

Equal pay for equal work isn't just a gender issue. The lifetime earnings of black and brown men lag behind those of their white male colleagues, as noted by the Pew Research Center. Research funded by the Department of Justice also shows that white male felons are more likely to be employed than black men with a bachelor's degree and no criminal record.

In order to make an inclusive and equitable workplace experience, companies must listen to, understand, and internalize the experiences of a diverse workforce. Doing so will help them analyze their practices to ensure that some employees aren't allowed to "fail upward" while others have to move mountains for a shot at getting ahead. Read on for stories of such mountain movers.

Orchid Bertelsen:
The Model Minority and Assimilation

Bärí A. Williams: What's unique about your background? Tell me about yourself.

Orchid Bertelsen: I work at Nestlé in the Innovation Group, which most people are surprised exists, because you tend to think of candy and ice cream. My grandparents met at KU [University of Kansas]. I'm the only person without a grad degree in my family.

I was born in Kansas but moved to Taiwan when I was two. Once I came back to the [United] States, I repeated first grade in a suburb of Chicago because there was concern that learning English was going to be an issue. In Asian culture, summer class is for getting ahead and having a head start on next year's topics. In the U.S., though, summer school is for catching up. So, my parents enrolled me in summer math class thinking I would learn the next year's topics. I went to a math class for summer school, and I was advanced, so they suggested I be put into a computer class. Once school restarted, I was the first Asian girl in these classes.

BAW: How has race affected your journey? What impact did it have on your sense of self as you transitioned through school and into the workplace?

OB: In college at George Washington, I had an ABC [American-born Chinese] boyfriend but didn't hang out with the international Asian students, a.k.a. FOBs [fresh off the boat]. I made those conscious decisions because my father wanted me to blend in and assimilate as best as possible. I also never felt like I belonged with the Taiwanese, because I didn't follow their customs and cultures.

This led to me not developing [an interest in the] history of my culture, a curiosity about my culture, and honestly, to not bringing that into the workplace. There was always the message of assimilation. Being the model minority is essentially white people pointing to you and saying, "Why can't you be like them? They are quiet, hardworking, and just happy to be here." The more you can be like everyone else, the more you will be treated like everyone else. Safety comes from blending in and not standing out.

I've never felt like I fit in anywhere. Subconsciously, proximity to whiteness might be why I married my husband, Eric. So, after marrying a white man, it was interesting to learn to be Taiwanese for my daughter. Due to all of these previous experiences, I wasn't interested in my heritage to that extent, and the workplace told me to embrace dominant culture and not my own. Even going to a Chinese restaurant or grocery store, I won't order in Chinese because I don't want to be judged.

There's a whole notion of identity and community and what that all means. It's frustrating that [my husband] can logically understand the idea of the privilege he has but never truly understand the full impact of it.

In Asian culture, the definition of beauty is still built upon white culture. You see skin-bleaching creams, double-eyelid surgery, eye-crease surgery, rhinoplasty, et cetera. It is all about how close to Asian you can look while still looking white.

BAW: How has being a "model minority" affected your career?

OB: The model-minority stereotype has positively impacted my career. Professionally, when I walk in the door, there's a certain amount of privilege that comes with being Asian. There are stereotypes with positive connotations—like you're good at math; you are docile, hardworking; you'll be quiet—and that can work to your advantage.

Part of the workplace burden is being Asian American—so there's the Asian part and then the American part. When it comes to both, I'm the worst type of perfectionist because I don't think I fully embody either. That manifests when I go back and look at something I've completed at work, and it can be excellent, but I'll dissect it to see how it can be better. That can be a gift and a curse. When you judge other people, it's a way of judging yourself. I'll look at someone's work and think, "Did you phone it in, or did you actually try?" It's like the adage, "If you want something done well, do it yourself." But there are different ways to get to a destination, and who is to say one way is better than another? But with this societal and cultural pressure of living up to this model minority, you're always putting yourself under a microscope. This is doubled when you're a woman in leadership. One misstep and it's like, "You set us all back." For example, Marissa Mayer—you can debate how well she did or not [as CEO of Yahoo], and yet I wondered if that means we as women were set back. It's the same pressure I feel, and fear, and it can manifest into worrying about if I'm not being a good enough employee and example of my race. And if I fail, am I setting us all back? Why am I carrying this weight when I don't have to?

Every single race has been profiled for one thing or another. When you look at the data and look at the facts, there is no real logical reaction to these things. When you look at male/female characteristics in the workplace, you can see how people can be viewed differently for the same traits. Like, if a man is assertive in the workplace, he has CEO qualities. If you have women who present that way, like Kamala Harris, or Elizabeth Warren, they are seen as emotional or too aggressive. Yet, Brett Kavanaugh was basically crying about how much he loved beer during a Supreme Court confirmation hearing, and no one disqualified him based on his emotions. It happens in every workplace, to some extent.

When I show up to a meeting or a presentation, I know that I need to have thought of every possible question and have answers for them and alternative solutions if people don't like the ones I suggest. I have to make sure I have all the data, no typos, backup data to back up my primary data, and an appendix that is maybe 48 slides.

It's good to keep things in proper context. You need to know the systems as they function today, especially in your own company, and the history of how they became that way so you can know the rules you're playing by—which can also tell us how to circumvent them. If you play by the boys' club rules, do you have to continue to perpetuate them in order to get other women ahead? Are you playing the long game or the short game? For women of color, this is especially important—for black women, [being assertive] is too direct and aggressive, and for Asian women, it is seen as completely out of character, and best to be passive.

I like the idea of the American Dream. We're fed the myth of the straight white male founder who did it all on his own. We know that isn't real, but people don't understand the structural, cultural, and systemic issues around how to achieve it. We weren't all born at the same starting point and it isn't really based on merit—so people should stop pretending it is. For me, the real American Dream is someone like Lil Nas X, who achieved success with everything working against him. And maybe the next great tech entrepreneur is some young woman in Ethiopia who has the odds stacked against her, who doesn't have great connections or Harvard to drop out of, so what does access look like for her?

Edwin Wong:
A Minority in a Majority-Minority Environment

Bärí A. Williams: What's unique about your background? Tell me about yourself.

Edwin Wong: I'm an LA [Los Angeles] native and currently SVP [senior vice president] of innovation at a media company.

I grew up in Highland Park in LA in the early 1990s. It was about 70 percent Latinx and 20 percent Asian, and the rest was split between black and white folks. It wasn't a wealthy environment. It was crime ridden. My high school yearbook had a page dedicated to people who were killed and didn't make it to the end of the year. My calculus class was shot up because students were fighting. I was mugged three or four times while walking home from school. When you go to a school like that and live in that environment, it humbles and grounds you when you make it. My dad was a working-class guy, and it made me appreciate my circumstances more.

My father was always dressed up when he was not in his baker's uniform. He wore slacks, a white shirt, and it was always tucked in. It was an example to me that I should be dressed in a certain way so people see that I'm professional. Whenever I'm out, I'm always going to be in a tie and a long-sleeved shirt and slacks. It's an homage to my dad, but it is also a show of respect for my position and those that I meet in that position.

BAW: How has race affected your journey? What impact did it have on your sense of self as you transitioned through school and into the workplace?

EW: I spent the early part of my life wishing in every environment that I could just survive. At school, how can I get through the day? At home, how can I not get in trouble? At college, how can I ensure I don't get put on academic probation? All the foundational parts of my life required me to comply, and I took a History of Christianity class, and this made me question what I was participating in based on how violent and inconsistent it was. The more I asked questions of the Christian value system, the more pushback I got about conforming. I just wanted answers, and I got more pleas to conform by my Cantonese family. When I shaved my head as my dad was going through cancer, he said, "You idiot. Why did you shave your head? You'll never get a good job because you look like a punk." Part of why I kept the bald head was a symbol against my dad to show him I did get a great corporate job in spite of his pronouncement.

Figuring out how to navigate through majority spaces, and especially in majority-minority spaces, is interesting. People presume that people of color will all get along, but that isn't necessarily the case since people will still self-segregate. Going to a predominantly Latinx school, I had to learn how to be a minority among minorities, and that gave me a greater appreciation for the experience of different people.

I learned how to navigate a space in which I was surrounded by a bunch of people that were all discriminated against. It almost became like a survival tactic—like code switching to traverse different people and places. Living in Highland Park, that experience helped me survive at Pomona College, because it was predominantly white. I was a psych major, and I didn't become a doctor or lawyer like other good Asian kids. Having this experience allowed me to read contexts, and to fit in and move in different spaces without hesitation or fear.

In my 20s, I realized that if I was going to fit in, I would do it on my terms. But when my dad died, I realized that none of this sh*t really matters. The reward feels better because I didn't have to comply or compromise in order to succeed. You still have to navigate parts of your identity and structural systems to compromise, but you can find a way to do it on your terms. This is particularly true when you're good at your job. If your output is good, there is little people can say to you about appearance or presentation in certain workplaces. If anything, it's just another motivating factor, because when you are your best self, you do your best work.

Being a minority in a majority-minority space gave me the ability to understand and relate to people on a basic, human level. It has always allowed me to connect with all sorts of people, I suppose, from management to the hourly workers. Connecting with people in this way, as opposed to connecting in a structural way, is really the difference. When you strip everything away, we are just people, and I truly believe that. So, me being in my position is just really a little bit of luck. When you come from the outside, you are able to see people holistically and can relate. It becomes something good because people rally around that relatability. We all just want that.

At work, that manifests in putting common goals and tasks at the forefront. That's what we all want—to contribute to our organization, and to ensure we are seen a contributor. I think being able to take my experience and relate to folks on a basic level allows for that. I don't have to focus so much on who I am and how I show up, so instead, I can shift that energy and attention to what I contribute and what that yields for the bottom line. It all levels out in the end.

Mark S. Luckie:
Black, Gay, and *Out*spoken in Tech

Bärí A. Williams: What's unique about your background? Tell me about yourself.

Mark S. Luckie: Being black and gay and navigating the workplace is definitely interesting. An interesting thing that people are taken aback by is me representing many underrepresented communities, not just black or gay people. I'm fighting for all.

BAW: How has race affected your journey? What impact did it have on your sense of self as you transitioned through school and into the workplace?

MSL: Working in tech and in journalism, I never wanted to be the token black guy. I went to mostly black schools, I went to an HBCU [historically black college and university], so when I get into these predominantly white spaces, they always want me to teach them "black things." I've been asked to teach coworkers how to twerk, how to do certain dances, and how to use slang terms.

I've never been my whole self at work. I'm from South Central [in Los Angeles]. The more relaxed I am, the more my slang gets relaxed. So, I'm aware that if I'm out here talking to people like the way I talk to my friends at home, or dressing how I would on weekends, it means people won't take me seriously. I actually overdressed when I worked at Twitter, specifically because you want to be better than the best-dressed person in the room. Button-downs, dress shoes, slacks—that was my uniform. Lots of people fight against respectability politics, but you have to play the game, to some extent.

A former colleague at Facebook was from Brooklyn, and he had the thickest accent. I remember he gave a presentation to a large group of us, and he sounded like Mr. Rogers. That accent was gone! It's natural for us to do this, but it's crazy to see it in action. Working in tech, I was always hyperaware when there were more than two or three of us [black colleagues] having a conversation because you get stares, and you know people are wondering, "What are they talking about? What are they planning?" It's a dual life for sure.

When I worked at Twitter, the office manager asked me to talk about what was going on in Ferguson at an all-office meeting, like an office town hall. There were less than 10 black people in the office, and there were about 300 employees in that building. From their perspective, they wanted someone to talk about this issue, and I'm black, so I could tell them what was going on. I had the thought, "If I don't do this, nobody else will do this." It was a large event, it was transforming the platform at the time, and Black Twitter was taking off. If I didn't do it, who would? It wasn't my role, but I decided to do it. I made sure to have metrics, and I had all the other black folks raise their hands, and I said, "Please engage them and ask questions, if they are open." For the rest of my career, I was radicalized by that moment. I realized how little people knew about the black community, even though the black community overindexes on Twitter and social media generally. It was interesting to note not only how little they knew but that they didn't appear to be curious or eager to find out on their own.

I never heard any acknowledgement of how Black Twitter was responsible for most trending topics, for actually providing free marketing for products, and how they were responsible for launching many trends, influencers, and products. The data was there, including data about which shows are most talked about. While analyzing it, you can see black women were responsible for most of those trends, without any credit or any just due.

Diversity isn't white women, and [focusing solely on white women] is what lots of diversity professionals pat themselves on the back for.

BAW: How does being a double minority—being both black and gay—affect your workplace experiences?

MSL: I toe the line of masculine and feminine. At work, I present more masculine. At Twitter, most people didn't know I was gay, and I never talked about my personal life. One, it wasn't anyone's business, and two, I was dating multiple people.

I didn't acknowledge my sexuality at Twitter until after Blackbirds (the black employee resource group) got organized and was successful. One thing I noticed about Twitter's gay employee resource group was that it was very white. I never felt accepted in that space. They didn't seem to find black people or people of color a priority. So, it seemed as if that intersectionality, being gay and of color, just wasn't something on their radar. That group was very focused on what they wanted to do, only, and not really looking to expand that view or other interests.

Black masculinity versus gay-perceived femininity is more of an issue with black colleagues than white colleagues, as it could completely change how people interact with you. I had to get used to having straight friends and talking to them about my fiancé at the time. With my history in tech, it was schooling black women: "No, I'm not going shopping with you. No, I'm not doing your hair. No, I'm not going to let you call me 'sis.'" It's about setting boundaries about what it means to be gay and black, and if you work in tech, you don't know a lot of black gays. I'll fix that for you.

Leah Wright-Rigueur:
Being a Young Black Woman in the Ivory Tower

Bärí A. Williams: What's unique about your background? Tell me about yourself.

Leah Wright-Rigueur: I'm an associate professor at an elite university, and prior to that I was an assistant professor at another university.

BAW: How has race affected your journey? What impact did it have on your sense of self as you transitioned through school and into the workplace?

LWR: My experience has been unique for a black woman in higher education. I've had a really fortunate experience in the academy. The problem is that my situation as a black woman in academia is that of an outlier, yet I still face some of the same significant issues that black women in higher education face, and that is troubling to me. One person having a seat at the table is better than nothing, but it's effectively meaningless. One person can't change an institution, and it's not a reflection of large transformation or significant change, particularly as it relates to racial or gender equity. The academy struggles with the notion of presence—[black women] are very rarely in positions of power, and we also aren't in high-ranking administrative positions or tenured positions, and those are essentially powerful and policy-making positions. In those roles, there are things we can do, but we don't have institutional power, and that's the larger issue. The rare individuals that are in these positions still face many of the same problems. The success of one individual does not erase the systemic racial and gender barriers for others.

We tend to think of the ivory tower as this really progressive, tolerant, liberal space. American academies generally *are*, especially if you look at metrics of people identifying as liberal. But when it comes to race and gender, the academy is conservative, and in some cases, regressive. In a lot of ways, racial and gender diversity is a symbolic gesture, and there aren't actually committed resources and support geared toward radically remaking the academy along racial, gender, and diverse lines.

Academic institutions have been at the forefront in terms of undergraduate efforts, with issues around LGBTQ+ rights, debt-free admission, and grants, but when it comes to faculty and staff, they are far more reluctant to do the necessary work in order to see a diverse rendering of the institution. The number of black faculty members in the academy is abysmal. It rivals STEM [science, technology, engineering, and mathematics] diversity-in-tech numbers. The number of tenured black faculty in prominent institutions is horrible.

As a black woman, I am hyperinvisible. Being both invisible and hypervisible feels like gaslighting. I'm asked to do labor that I'm not compensated for, and at the same time I'm ignored in other realms. It can be confusing, because then people don't know how to interact with me: "Do you want us to leave you alone, or do you want us to give you more attention?" It's really more of a desire for people to respect and engage me as a scholar and a colleague, as opposed to being just seen as an available resource. I've constantly heard other black women in the academy talk about this.

I made a decision very early on in my career to focus on my career. Rather than focusing on lines in the sand that seem arbitrary, different rules for different people, things that seem out of reach—I made the choice to focus on things I can do for self, and self-preservation, in terms of my sanity. That has worked to the benefit of the institution I've worked for every time. Focusing on the things that I can control, in addition to sitting on committees, speaking up, and doing diversity work, this is what has preserved my ability to remain in the academy. There is a level of freedom, and I use that word carefully and cautiously, with working for the institution for nine months, and then there are three months where we still work for the institution, but we can do work on our own. I have the ability to live as authentically as I can, given these flexible boundaries.

For some of my colleagues, and this isn't unique to the institutions I worked for, they struggle to understand the boundaries that I've set between myself and the institution. I was judged for things that I perceived to be done based upon my authentic self, or who I am— how I dress, hair, family members, gender. There was one instance in which I turned down a tenured offer from an institution to accept my role at Harvard, to which a colleague made a joke by saying, "We got you for cheap, ha ha!" I had a discussion with a colleague about invisible-hypervisible struggles, and she suggested I cut my hair, as it's too long to be deemed professional. Another colleague asked about how much money I spend on clothes. I've had student evaluations where they have commented on my age, saying I look too young to be knowledgeable, questioning my credentials, my body, among other things. The worst student evaluation said, "She's an idiot, and not sure about her pedigree. My mom knows more than she does, but she has a hot rack, and I'd love to bang her." Now, consider this is a qualitative component with a numerical value that is used for promotional and tenure evaluation.

Then there are colleagues who ignore me, never engage me, don't come to my events, haven't read my work, nor discussed me with students, but have plenty to say when it comes time to evaluate me.

After repeated interactions with colleagues, staff, and also students, I made the decision that for the academy to get the best of me, I had to set parameters around how the academy could interact with me. The boundary aspect, particularly for black women, is something that isn't unusual. Black women are coined as mean professors, hostile, standoffish; we tend to get poor student evaluations, so we tend to wear a mask in public so as to combat some of that narrative. I have to be aware of the number of students I take on in addition to the students I'm required to advise and take on, how often are my office hours, how often am I seen on campus, et cetera. The balancing act you are constantly working through, and the weight you walk into work with is something the majority of your colleagues don't have to think of.

BAW: What are the steps an institution can take to address and alleviate that situation?

LWR: This is where the academy loses its way. This is, however, where I can do the most good. If I have an event and 500 people show up, including upper-level staff, and they see real engagement around issues of race and politics, it meets the demands of the students—the customers—and it goes a long way with administration thinking through some of these broader institutional questions.

I have to have an optimistic outlook about career that recognizes my privilege and how fortunate I've been, and that I'm an outlier, while also accepting my frustrations with the broader academy and institutions generally. Two identities at war, constantly trying to be reconciled in the same body. The only conscious decision I can make is to focus on what I can do to live as close as I can to preserving my authentic self. I can be grateful for where I am and still realize my path has been full of potholes, and some of those potholes aren't unique to me, and are applicable to black women across industries. It manifests in a multitude of ways, and people choose to deal with this duality in very different ways. Some thrive, some disassociate, some compartmentalize, some become cynical, some hoard resources, and some reinvest and commit to changing the institution. Each of those people are saying something, and they are saying it loudly. There have to be decisive, transformative decisions made to shift the paradigm at these institutions. Listen to what your employees are saying, and then do something about it.

It has only made me better going into work every day being unapologetically who I am. Even if the institution has struggled with it, it has still made the institution better for it.

How do you both navigate the sense, "you should be grateful [for being here]" and then deal with colleagues that have no sense of that same feeling, and think you should just be happy to be here? How do you reconcile success and the path to get there, with all of the bumps in the road along the way—significant bias; discriminatory, institutionalized barriers—and how do you smooth the path to make it easier for others?

"We are committed to diversity." The solutions have to be rooted in acknowledging institutional deliberate actions, so we need to take deliberate actions to correct it. It really takes visionary leadership in order to get to that place.

Dr. Anonymous:
Advocacy as a Black Female Doctor

Bärí A. Williams: What's unique about your background? Tell me about yourself.

Dr. Anonymous: I'm a black woman doctor from the Midwest. I'm an OB-GYN, and I'm also working on diversity as it pertains to patient health advocacy.

BAW: How has race affected your journey? What impact did it have on your sense of self as you transitioned through school and into the workplace?

DA: The reason I went into OB-GYN was because I felt like I could relate more and create a different environment for myself later in life. There were days in medical school and residency where I was the only black woman there. That led to me deciding that OB-GYN made sense. Surgery was highly toxic and male dominated, and on the borderline of being a #MeToo moment if I chose that specialty. My gender and experiences of being the only woman and being the only black woman is why I chose to be an OB-GYN. Our field is dominated by women, and the empowerment of having that advantage is nice. Women are requesting female providers, and it's another privilege, but how I got there evolved over time because of feeling "Othered," or different, or not having a voice in the operating room. There have been episodes when I've been at a conference, and someone will repeat a comment I said and they get the credit, and I have to say, "Hey, I just said that." You are routinely discounted in some spaces because women aren't "loud" with their comments and we aren't expected to be or rewarded for it.

I initially came to the Bay Area for residency, and I planned to return to the Midwest or the East Coast when my residency ended. But people kept saying, "Well, you are really good at public speaking. You are good about organizing people and things. People like you, and you should be chief of this department."

That was my big opportunity to have more visibility, and people got to know who I was throughout the region. Once our medical group appointed a new CEO, the group posited the idea to invest in this space with culturally responsive care and inclusion, and they wanted a doctor to facilitate it from the physician's point of view. When you are dealing with caregivers and patients, it is slightly different. Now, we're building a team, getting the engagement of physicians already involved in the space, and articulating our goals clearly.

I think it's a privilege to bring the voice of patients who are voiceless. They go through back doors to find me. Once we meet, we have these amazing conversations about how they have experienced care, and the struggles with communication within health care, the health literacy piece, with fear and trust. For the most part, being a woman, especially in this specialty, is what helps the most—because I'm relatable. So, being a woman in this space, and in this medical group, has been a benefit. But sometimes, there are just certain barriers because it may not be something in my language and culture. I tell patients I'm not in the office every day because I'm advocating for them in a different way, and that requires me to be at headquarters. It is me using a different part of my brain. But I go back to the office and I hear these stories, and I know this is a unique position for me to be in because I do have the lived experience to understand what some of these people are navigating and going through. I can relate from college and being discouraged from advocating for myself.

There are advantages to working in an urban area, because it's culturally and ethnically diverse with both the workforce and the patients, and it's why I chose to work at this particular hospital group as opposed to other places. The unicorn experience I have is that there are several other black women doctors who also work with me, and we are relatively close. It's a great sense of camaraderie and support, particularly when navigating the workplace. One night, we all met up for dinner and we had on matching T-shirts. This white woman came up to us, as a collective group of black women wearing "Black Doctors" shirts, and she told us she was a doctor, too; her specialty; and how she had never seen anything like this, and she celebrated it!

I made sure to place myself in environments to thrive. It is why I have designed my career to be in particular environments and spaces to be able to have a certain type of experience. In college, I had a 3.5 [GPA] in the school of engineering, and the dean suggested I try nursing, or something else, because he didn't think I'd get into medical school. That was a spark he lit, so that I was motivated to prove him wrong. I got into several schools. I applied for postbaccalaureate programs, in case, and I got into those.

The pipeline is hard because people discount the importance of having a mentor on this journey. That also is key when you are working somewhere—the importance of mentors and sponsors in the workplace. I learned that the hard way in high school and college, because people will try to steer you in a direction they believe you are capable of, not based on your actual ability. There are so many barriers going into medicine, and I was fortunate that my parents found a way to get me involved in summer programs related to medicine, to get study courses for me. How you navigate your way into medicine is often done by the student on their own, and they have to figure it out, which may be discouraging, but it does inspire grit and resiliency.

SOMEONE CALLED ME A RACIST. HOW DO I RESPOND?

First, though difficult, try not to take that feedback personally. Instead, direct your energy toward self-reflection, and try to understand what about your words and actions may have led a colleague to that conclusion. Were you inarticulate? Did you have good intentions, but your delivery was poor? Second, talk to your colleague about what you may have said or done to make them feel slighted and come to that conclusion. Perhaps it was just a misunderstanding in the message you intended to deliver and how it was received. As long as both parties are open to dialogue and willing to have the conversation in the spirit of understanding, common ground can be reached. Finally, think about how you would approach the situation differently and how you would convey your message if given the opportunity to do it over again.

Key Takeaways

- When engaging with someone, be mindful of how *they* choose to identify. We often identify people based upon markers such as race as opposed to how they want to be seen. Take, for example, someone who is part of a minority group due to race, but who is also differently abled. Being differently abled may be more central to their identity than their race, for instance. Additionally, word choice is significant. Some people like the term *Latinx*, whereas others prefer *Hispanic* or to be identified by their country of origin. Race is often the biggest identifying marker we use to categorize someone. Be intentional and cognizant of how you engage with someone around topics of race, particularly their own.

- Before engaging in a conversation or offering an opinion on a controversial topic, ask yourself if you're basing any of your opinions solely on stereotypes or preconceived notions.

- Word choice matters, particularly around topics of race or when engaging with colleagues of a different race. There are certain words, phrases, and terms that are rife with hidden meaning. For example, "aggressive" when speaking of black women can be seen as coded negative language. "Docile," "demure," and "soft-spoken" may have different connotations when speaking of Asian women or men. Be aware of your language.

- Not all compliments are equal. When praising a colleague for a workplace win, be aware of what you say. For instance, don't congratulate a person of Asian descent for being a good public speaker "despite having an accent." That qualification is a backhanded compliment that does more harm than good. It indicates low expectations of someone's ability, which puts them at a disadvantage.

PART TWO

WOMEN: UNDERAPPRECIATED, UNDERPAID, AND OVERWORKED

Women are often subject to second-class citizenship as they work toward professional success. Even when they gain positions of power, women are regularly judged on everything from how "nice" they are to how willing they are to take on the emotional baggage of their colleagues. For many women, interactions with men in the workplace can be fraught with anxiety due to unequal pay, sexual harassment, and the struggle to champion themselves while remaining "likable."

There is no shortage of stories about men behaving badly in a variety of industries. Some high-profile examples are the sexual harassment scandals involving Fox News CEO Roger Ailes and film director Harvey Weinstein. Sexual harassment exposed by Ellen Pao and Susan Fowler in the tech industry helped feed the #MeToo movement. The "Me Too" phrase, which was coined by black female activist Tarana Burke in 2006, has became the rallying cry for women in the workplace to unabashedly share their stories of harassment and assault.

Women in the workplace face complex problems and many are the result of intersectionality, whether it involves sexuality, familial status, age, race, or religion. Navigating multiple identities, juggling personal and professional life, and figuring out how to excel at work are just some of the challenges that women have been required to master.

Rani Molla:
Impostor Syndrome, Race, Gender, Economic Status, and Creativity

Bärí A. Williams: What's unique about your background? Tell me about yourself.

Rani Molla: I'm a journalist and reporter covering tech at *Vox*. Reporting on a space that is largely white, male, and wealthy has been a trip, and it takes constant affirmation externally and internally to pull it off.

Why even cover that space? Because I'm interested in it, and there's so much potential. I remember when I first got a computer, and I love the potential that it supports for a meritocracy. The potential is still there.

I grew up with no advantages at all—with homelessness, living in a segregated community in Long Island, and no food sometimes. Being young, brown, and poor all melded together for me, and I thought I deserved those things because that is what society mirrors back to me. It was my own way of rationalizing the inequality in my life. In order to make things not complete chaos, you try to rationalize why this all happened to you.

Then you go to tech. In a different way, you still aren't there, especially since there is ridiculous wealth on display. You see that, and it makes you scared. The prior experiences of life made me intimidated, and it's just another reinforcement that you don't belong. For a long time, when I had good ideas, I just considered them my own, and probably not interesting, so I didn't share them.

It's like suspending disbelief. I try to make all the thoughts go away that make me think, "You don't belong. Why are you here? This isn't for you." I have to suspend that fear and put distance there. It's me making myself be more forward thinking instead of backward looking, which is what makes me feel like I shouldn't be there in the first place. I know I'm here because I belong here, but even with imposter syndrome, it's a motivator. I also try to take it as a given—I'm here now. Now what? I don't know how useful imposter syndrome is anymore, because after a while, you've proven yourself again and again. When you're younger, you create mechanisms to deal with your life, and after a while, they don't work anymore. But in those ways, it did drive me, and it got me here, but I don't need that needling voice telling me I'm not good enough because I *know* I am, or I wouldn't be here. You only have so much capacity, and I want to fill it with the concepts I'm writing on, what I'm covering, and how I handle those things productively. If you don't push yourself or go to these things outside of your realm of possibility, you are safer. My biggest asset is my mind. So, I'm trying to be 100 percent there. You have to use as much of that capacity as you can, and that little voice is just sapping energy and is a distraction. But you aren't better for it. I would rather challenge myself, so I quiet and appease that voice.

BAW: How has gender affected your journey? What impact did it have on your sense of self as you transitioned through school and into the workplace?

RM: When I got to college at Oberlin, I was struck by how much everyone already knew. My awareness of the world was different: I didn't have the right references or the same manners, or know the right people, and I didn't read the right books. It's like learning the language of rich white people. It is much the same in writing about tech: There are terms thrown around in tech, and acronyms, and you become aware of what you don't know. There's no reason why I shouldn't know as much as they do, but there is always this awareness of Otherness.

Along the way, there were lots of people who were allies and believed in me and saw something in me before I recognized it. What's been most interesting is that "I get it," but I also offer a completely different viewpoint than someone else because of my unique journey and qualifications. It makes me better in a lot of ways. I can take that skill set and bring it to bear on technology, what I'm reporting on, and the importance of it. When I do find the right words, and am most authentically myself, I feel like it resonates with people in a great way.

The people who created the technology that I report on had good intentions, and I see myself as a protector of that. Tech is supposed to make our lives better and safer, and make work less onerous and more efficient. Those are the missions they promised. I feel like through my work, I have to keep people honest and hold their feet to the fire with implementing these promises through their work and their products. So, in some ways, we are in service of each other but also at odds. I can make people think about things they don't want to, or wrongdoings they won't acknowledge, but it forces them to make changes or at least acknowledge they need change. Are you *really* making the world a better place—is the net benefit of this *really* a net benefit? It's a discussion we are all having together.

This is also the future. This is where things are going. It's the Wild West out here. There are no regulations, and so we [journalists] are the ones trying to keep people and products in check and ensure social mores are in place and not dismissed in the pursuit of this technology. Journalists are doing what we do—nitpicking and taking things apart— but it's a larger conversation about where the future goes. Too many futures have been written without me. This time I'm at the table, and I want to see my fingerprints on what comes out of it.

So, it's hard now, but it's been much harder, and I'm much more comfortable now. You get used to comfort very quickly, but I try to remember something may hurt or make me insecure in the moment; I put things in perspective. Still, every day, I get to go into a beautiful, well-designed office with air conditioning and eat anything I want, and come up with ideas that I think are interesting, and find the words for them. I'm living the dream even when it sucks.

If we actually can keep tech egalitarian, to ensure [tech companies and the people who run them] don't give into vices, then it won't be as difficult for someone else to move into this space later. They can just walk through the door, and the goal is to pay it forward. We just unionized at *Vox*, so we made it a rule that 50 percent of the candidates have to come from a marginalized background—gender, race, ability, sexuality. *Vox* is more diverse than anywhere I've worked, and similarly, the ideas bandied about and stories published are also the most interesting. It's hard to not notice the things that are missing. I come in to work, and I'm not the Other. It matters that I'm not the only woman, that I can say what I want and it isn't a big deal.

Morgan Debaun:
Life as a CEO and Culture Creator

Bärí A. Williams: What's unique about your background? Tell me about yourself.

Morgan Debaun: I'm the cofounder and CEO of Blavity, which is a lifestyle platform bringing people together through community, events, and education.

BAW: How has gender affected your journey? What impact did it have on your sense of self as you transitioned through school and into the workplace?

MD: Initially, before Blavity, I was a PM [product manager] at a large tech company, and I then went into business development at the company after college at Washington University in St. Louis, where I'm from. While I was a PM, I had a really fun team; they were very experienced, and they were able to self-manage. That defused challenges I may have had. My peer group was the harder part: being a representative of that product, among other PMs jockeying for resources. I was 23 years old working at a big company where people had 20-plus years' experience, so I'm sure there were things I said without proper context. I realized I didn't want to be in a tech company as the highest-ranking black woman at 26. I knew there was more to life. I didn't want to be extraordinary just for existing.

I kept it quiet when I figured out what I wanted to do. I set a disciplined schedule for myself to make sure I had time dedicated to my "project"—at the time it was a project, not a company. That was mostly nights and weekends. I was giving myself six months to work on it intensely, and during those six months, I was going to remove distractions—going out, spending money. I saved money so I could live in [San Francisco] for a year. I set clear goals and a clear timeline. I didn't set goals as to where the community needed to be, but I knew I wanted to quit my day job to work on it full-time. So, I focused on what I needed to do to quit. Reconciling that with my day job, my perspective at work changed once I figured out I wanted to quit. People spend time at work thinking about what people think of them when they are focused on an upward trajectory. When I removed the desire to advance and just focused on getting work done, I actually wound up saving a lot of time.

BAW: How have your lived experiences and previous work experiences been influential in building your own company culture?

MD: Blavity is a majority-black company, but that's also based on our mission. When it comes to other people applying, anyone can, and I feel like in the interview process, people prefilter. If you apply, it's lit! If I give you a behavioral or case study and you do the work, you've opted in. We are unapologetic about who we are and who we serve. So, if you are down with providing black joy and happiness by spreading information and curating content and experiences, then great! If you embrace the mission, it's fine.

When it comes to hiring, we've made a lot of mistakes. It's interesting how much a mission-driven company can create space and desire for people to work at a media company that wouldn't normally consider it. We do behavioral interviews, and people want to be here for fun but may not want to do the work. So, we make the interview process labor-intensive. There are case studies and spreadsheets, and you have to demonstrate that you can do the work.

We create an inclusive environment so you don't have to be black to feel included here. Plus, Blavity is just a reminder that everyone has their own story, and we're mostly people of color here, but we're still all different. Some are Haitian, some went to an HBCU, some are mixed. The color is important, but the actual person is more important. Each person is many different things.

As far as fostering an inclusive atmosphere, in a lot of ways it happens naturally, because we don't think about it all day every day. Maybe I'm biased as the CEO, but I think we don't spend a lot of time doing cultural competency workshops. It just happens through natural conversation. But that comes through having an environment where people feel comfortable to be themselves. We encourage them to be who they are here. Some want to do squat challenges or set up fitness boards in the office. Other people make plans for trying new restaurants. It feels comfortable and personal here. It's a workplace; people should be comfortable here, but it's still a workplace. There is a value that needs to be here, so that's where sometimes it can get confusing. But as the CEO, I have to set the parameters. And I'm me, and that's not changing, and if someone has a problem with it, that isn't my problem.

Aubrey Blanche:
Choosing Your Battles as a Diversity Professional

Bärí A. Williams: What's unique about your background? Tell me about yourself.

Aubrey Blanche: From a high-level view of what identities I wear versus the one that people put on me, it would be Latina, queer, disabled, and woman. "Woman" is how people identify me the most, and it's what I identify with the least. As a diversity professional, the way that I think about the work that I do is building justice and fairness in the world, because capitalism is one of the biggest drivers, and you have to change things from the inside. I do this work inside of companies because I believe how I present it makes it easier for me to do that work, and with the tech industry broadly, I'm able to pass as a white woman. I have more resilience because of my certain privileges, so I do that work for others.

BAW: How has gender affected your journey? What impact did it have on your sense of self as you transitioned through school and into the workplace?

AB: The interesting thing is being a femme person is more salient than my biological woman-ness. I've been told I can't be good at tech, but is that because I'm a woman or Latina or what? But I enjoy being femme, because it is a blatant "f*ck you" factor in this industry and I would like to prove that you're wrong.

I think all of us who are underrepresented play a strategic calculus game at work. For me, my job scope is to create change, so I find I can be more conservative in terms of the way I deal with structural and cultural sexism. So, I'm less likely to push on issues around my gender because I'm visibly a woman, but it has less effect on my passing identities and could also harm the work forward on an enterprise level. I have to pick sometimes: Do I advocate for the group or myself? Because you have a finite amount of capital in the workplace, and you have to choose when, where, and how to spend it. So, I push on issues around race at work because I'm a white-passing person, so I have the ability to do that and be listened to, more so than doing that as a woman and not jeopardizing the programs and issues that I'm championing inside.

As much as being a queer person is a salient thing in how I present and conduct my life, the LGBTQ+ stuff at work is that I don't have to burn any capital on that around inclusivity. There isn't a lot of change management, but there is the ability to be more inclusive, whereas with gender and race, there is still a lot of work to do.

I was a first-generation college student, and I went to undergrad at Northwestern. I was so alienated by how entitled my classmates were about having access and incredible opportunities to attend a university like that. It was exacerbated going to Stanford for my PhD. It was just a reminder that people aren't aware of how marginalized people have to work twice as hard for access to those opportunities. It was enough sexism and racism, and I didn't see a way to make myself successful in that system. But then I went and joined tech and couldn't find other minorities.

I dropped out of Stanford due to systemic sexism and racism, and didn't think I could succeed. So, when I got to tech, I was confused and wondering, "Where are all the Mexicans?" And what spurred me into D&I [diversity and inclusion] work was solving my own problem. Doing that work means you are quadrupling your own sense of oppression—and do you have the coping mechanisms to do that? It requires 10 different group chats that are women of color hyping each other up, a strong therapy system, daily self-care practice, and a strong family. It feels like a lot of responsibility because I am responsible for someone's employee experience.

People also discount me because I'm a five-foot-tall, bug-eyed woman, and people just presume I won't be confident *or* competent. People assume that HR professionals just won't be as sharp as engineers, which is a terrible assumption. Because I engineer people-based systems instead of computers, that doesn't make me automatically deficient. There are so many brilliant people in this industry that are talked down to and believe and internalize it, and then it's really about some "tech bros'" own personal deficiencies, and maybe they just aren't good at seeing talent.

There have been a couple of times in workplace networking situations where someone will discuss something and then discount me and say, "This is too technical for you." I can code in Python and other languages because I do data analysis. There's an assumption that because I'm a woman in HR, I couldn't possibly have technical skills. It isn't that these women aren't talented; it's that you don't know how to properly assess talent.

It is hard to do this work sometimes and be assumed to be a white woman, because it can come across as a bit like white saviorism, but

I'm not white, and we have to be able to be mindful to not ostracize people that want to, and can, help. Especially now that I've dedicated my life to advancing the interests of my community, it's a pity that we're eating our own and contributing to isolation of people that actually want to help. Every one of my friends who pass, they also experience this, and they fear the isolation of having visible people of color tell you to "shut the f*ck up and don't complain about your white privilege."

But I believe that underrepresented people are brilliant, and the systems we have to measure that brilliance, particularly in the workplace, are broken and insufficient. The problem isn't the people—it's the rigid systems they are forced to operate within. I've had great privileges and a certain level of access, so I'm ready to dismantle these systems.

Rael Nelson James:
Culture Shock as a Black Woman in Nonprofits and Philanthropy

Bärí A. Williams: What's unique about your background? Tell me about yourself.

Rael Nelson James: I'm a cishet black woman, working in nonprofits and philanthropy for the majority of my career in various roles, and now I work for a nonprofit in a diversity capacity.

BAW: How has gender affected your journey? What impact did it have on your sense of self as you transitioned through school and into the workplace?

RNJ: Working in nonprofits, the bulk of the workforce in the organizations I've worked for have been mostly women. They are primarily white women, and sometimes it's great and easy to find common ground, and sometimes it's a bit harder because of the nature of how we each came to work in these spaces. For me, it is an extension of my childhood, and how I was raised, and for some of them, it stems from wanting to give back, or feeling the *need* to give back, and how that translates into this work.

Relationships at work are very important to me. Even the places where I had "work friends," I had a profound sense of loneliness at work. Let me be clear: They aren't real friends; they are work friends. When it comes to the people I would choose to go to lunch with, I would usually find another black woman, and it's like the same tool kit you used in college to find other black women, and it's an extension of that. In particular, this happened when the workplaces were predominantly white and the primary beneficiaries were black and brown.

There were times when I'd be at a gala for the organization I work for, and the only black people I'd see there would be me and someone onstage telling their story of how the organization helped them for the benefit of white funders to understand how their money is used, and I would ask myself, "How am I on the side of the people in the room who are funding when I actually relate more to the person onstage?" It can make you feel dirty—and of all the ways to feel about working, that's what I *don't* want it to do! Am I being used by white senior leadership because I'm seen as a bridge? Yes, I'm a woman, and that automatically gives me a certain level of credence and credibility in nonprofit work because we are viewed as nurturing, uplifting, and wanting to help. But then add my race on top of that, and it's like I'm a bridge between both worlds. That can be great, but it can also be a moment of self-reflection. You pay a price—a soul price—to get the check. Do I want to do this to get my check?

The older I've gotten and the longer I've been in the workforce, the more I've learned to read people professionally. You learn where your interests are aligned, and find authentic connections and then strategical alliances in the workplace. Unless someone is truly racist or whatnot, it is in their best interest to work well with you, or you make it in their best interest to work well with you. You do that by being likable, due to your access or proximity to power in the organization or whatever the reason is to have folks find affinity toward you. Times I haven't felt "in-group" is when I clearly wasn't the right fit. People are hardwired for "sorting," as the way we navigate information, groups of things, people, places, and situations. There are so many cultural messages we get to be around people who are like us—so, being a woman makes it easier to an extent, but because I'm not a white woman of a certain socioeconomic status, that makes it harder.

It is interesting to note that it has felt comfortable when people are very aware of their privilege and how to use it to advance the work, and not whispering about it as an aside. It's about harnessing your power and privilege to move the ball forward and how to effectively help marginalized people. That is what the sector is grappling with now, which was not the conversation 10 years ago.

Everybody in my family does some sort of social-impact work, so this was always sort of a given to me. Like, corporate? What's that? It was never on my radar. It was always a given that I would go into a field that helps the community. My mom is an artist and an actor, and she did activist work in prisons where they were teaching incarcerated folks to write plays to tell their stories. I'm still searching for the utopian view of the sector that I was introduced to as a child, because I know what it's capable of. But it is odd to take white funders on a tour of a school and then feel self-conscious and weird about that dynamic. You have to be aware of what people expect of you based on their interactions with you and their perceptions and preconceived notions of who you are or should be, based on cultural cues. One of the things that feels unfair, in the space we are in, is asking white people to learn more about race so it'll make more of us feel like we can have a fair shot and ownership over the workplace but there is so much pushback on that—and yet we've been learning about white people since birth, and that is the societal norm and every media narrative we get. They, in comparison, are not casually confronted with black people, blackness, and culture, where it would benefit all of us. The more exposure we get to cultures before we get into a situation to collaborate or do shared work for a goal, the better. For marginalized people to explain their humanity and cultural awareness is a very heavy burden, and it is unpaid labor. These are essential conversations, but it creates more of a burden on people of color, and that's the last thing they need.

Race is only one way that we are bound by community. I'm a third-generation college graduate. So, I don't have the same struggle as someone who grew up in poverty, and that is something that would be conflated in my workplace. Because I'm racially the same as our beneficiaries, that means I must have the same life story and experience of those we are helping. That's also a funny piece of being a black woman in nonprofits. There are middle-class black people. There are wealthy black people. I don't have the life experience to speak on what it's like growing up in the projects or having a certain socioeconomic experience. So, here in [Washington] DC, *white* is synonymous with *middle class* and everything up, including *wealthy* and including *generational wealth*. That's what is interesting about the city. You see the spectrum of socioeconomic wealth in blacks in DC and northern Virginia and parts of Maryland, and yet when you think of white people, you only see wealth.

Far more black women aspire to the C-suite [than reach it], but structural barriers lock people out. Part of [overcoming those barriers] is being able to build the right relationships—how to do it, make them authentic relationships, and to do it without sacrificing self. It's a delicate dance.

Laura I. Gomez:
The Tech Industry's Haves and Have-Nots

Bärí A. Williams: What's unique about your background? Tell me about yourself.

Laura I. Gomez: I'm the founder of Atipica, which is HR and candidate enterprise software. We sell B2B [business-to-business] software to source diverse candidates and match them to open roles in your system.

I'm a Mexican woman in tech, and was previously undocumented, which is a unique place to be.

BAW: How has gender affected your journey? What impact did it have on your sense of self as you transitioned through school and into the workplace?

LIG: In [Silicon] Valley, a lot of people get to fail up, especially white males. I have never had that luxury at any point in life. I was raised in Silicon Valley, but we came here from Mexico. My mother has been a nanny and a house cleaner for over 25 years, including to some tech CEOs, so I've seen what tech can give you, and I also know what it's like to not have that. None of the people my mom worked for ever once asked if her kids would be interested in the industry or offered an internship. But I got an internship with Hewlett-Packard. No one looked like me, and I hated it; it turned me off and made me want to get out of tech. But I've never felt like that was an option.

I've been in tech since I was 17. I had my first internship at Hewlett-Packard and then went and studied in college. I didn't really focus on computer science because I felt a lot of the imposter syndrome. After college, I joined a lot of early-stage tech companies all at various stages of growth. While working at them, I saw a need for more diversity.

I talk to women and they note that they feel the same pressure to be resilient and succeed. I know Morgan [Debaun, CEO of Blavity] has gotten a lot of money, and then you get other token people getting money, and they think the funding problem is fixed. The opportunity to fail—you see a lot of these founders who get pushed out, and they have an opportunity to fail. We don't get that as women of color, and even more so, black women. There is no opportunity or privilege to fail. If you're anyone that isn't a white man in this industry and in the Valley, you have to push through. You don't get a second shot.

There's a Latina who works in corporate, and we were having a discussion one morning and she said, "You have to overcompensate for being a Latina. And you have to succeed, because if you fail, we all fail." It needs to be emphasized [that only some people] have the privilege of failure. I'm sleep-deprived, trying to provide for my family, and tend to self-care, but we aren't afforded that luxury—the opportunity to be okay with saying, "Hey, I want to give up"—and that isn't allowed either, as a Latina founder or any founder of color.

I do believe that it is very hard for people who grew up in the Bay Area to watch an industry that has displaced people or to see local communities being pushed out, especially as minorities. We also don't have the privilege of ignoring the impact of people who grew up here and to see how they are affected by the rise of this industry and who it is for. I love the Bay Area, but I hate Silicon Valley—one, based on geography, and one is based on industry.

I may not be actively coding, but I'm more capable than other founders at looking at and using the data around hiring for the work-force that is reflective of demographics of the country, let alone the world. But a lot of VCs [venture capitalists] are white men, and if [being a white man] isn't your lived experience, your skill and vision are discounted. How are you thinking about inclusion, in particular? How are you building these products, and who are you building them for, and with? Why can't inclusion include the different types of inter-sectionality that encompass the lives of people of color and women, particularly as caregivers?

But white male founders are focused on other things, and I see that all the time. For instance, I went to [the reception for] Cloud 100, which is a *Forbes*-sponsored list noting the top 100 cloud-based tech companies. If you look at that list, the majority of the CEO recipients are men. There were only a handful of women that I saw at the reception. When I would come up to a group of men—let's say there were five of them—two of them would walk away, and they'd only walk away when they saw my tag. It didn't say CEO; it just had my name, but that was enough to dissuade them from engaging in discussion. People just discounted the ability that I may have something worthwhile to say or that I was worth knowing.

I also look at how people seem to think that women founders should be consumer-based in the tech industry. And it's hard to see a woman CEO dealing with enterprise business. When female founders are profiled, they are typically white women, and they do consumer-based products, like Wing, Rent the Runway, and Bumble. But being a Latina founder in enterprise makes it harder on every front: for fundraising, for peers to take you seriously, and to even build and sell the product. I don't feel like I can even rest because of the pressure to not fail for other black and Latina women—and the fact that we don't want [other] people to have the last word. I don't want a VC to have the last word on my viability as a Latina woman founder and my lived experience and what and how it matters. We don't give people the privilege to have the last word in terms of what we're building, specifically as women of color. It's not about me anymore but about whether we allow VCs and companies to have the last word on my success and whatever that success may mean.

WHAT QUALIFIES AS SEXUAL HARASSMENT?

Sexual harassment takes two forms: hostile work environment and quid pro quo. *Hostile work environment* means any words or actions with a sexual connotation that interfere with an employee's ability to work or that create an uncomfortable atmosphere. A hostile work environment can be created through sharing pictures and memes, making "jokes," or asking questions about someone's personal life or sexual experiences. What is important to note is that a hostile work environment can be created and felt even if these actions are not directed at a particular person. All that is required is to make the environment sexually charged and uncomfortable.

Quid pro quo is a type of sexual harassment that is seen as an even exchange. The literal Latin translation of the phrase is "this for that." This type of sexual harassment occurs when a superior or someone in a position of power, leverages their power over an individual to demand sexual favors in exchange for job benefits.

Key Takeaways

- The experience of being a woman in the workplace is as multi-faceted as the women who inhabit it. Keep in mind that there are certain identities that some women may prioritize over their gender—such as their race, sexual orientation, religion, or socio-economic status. Depending on the topic of conversation, the task at hand, or both, one of these identities may be more relevant than another at any given time.

- As we touched on in the introduction, gender is often erroneously conflated with sex assignment. They are not synonymous. To that point, how women express their gender identity can vary widely. "Feminine" expression is usually welcome, whereas "masculine" expression is not. One's self-identified gender and expression of that gender should be respected.

- When speaking about women in the workplace, people tend to think of the "average" woman as white. It is important to note that every woman's experience is not the same, particularly when it comes to intersectionality.

- Women are still struggling for equal pay in the workplace. On average, women have to work an extra four months to earn the same pay that men earn in one year. The difference is even greater for black, Native American, and Latina women.

PART THREE

LGBTQ+: AMERICA'S LAST PROTECTED CLASS IN THE WORKPLACE

Like all marginalized groups, the LGBTQ+ population—those who identify as lesbian, gay, bisexual, transgender, queer, asexual, intersex, or questioning—regularly deal with discrimination.

People within the LGBTQ+ spectrum often speak of the chameleon-like ability they adopt to hide their true selves so they can function in their professional lives and society as a whole. It's a learned behavior born of necessity and self-preservation. Without proper legal protections in place, LGBTQ+ people are subject to discrimination in the workplace without any repercussions for the colleagues or employers who discriminate.

The good news is that the LGBTQ+ community is continuing to become a more visible part of the public conversation, and societal notions of gender are beginning to shift as more and more people recognize gender identity as a spectrum. This recognition is changing the way we approach the idea of equal rights for all. The long-standing presence of transgender people is finally becoming more visible, and notions of gender itself are transforming.

Mike Rognlien:
LGBTQ+ Status as Truth and Strength

Bärí A. Williams: What's unique about your background? Tell me about yourself.

Mike Rognlien: I'm an out, proud, gay man, and I've been an HR executive for formal conservative banks to tech companies. The last company I worked for was Facebook, prior to launching my own HR training and diversity consulting company, Multiple Hats Management.

BAW: How has your gender identity, gender expression, or sexuality affected your journey? What impact did it have on your sense of self as you transitioned through school and into the workplace?

MR: When you talk about people who are wanting to be around diverse groups of people, you think back to patterns you've seen in childhood. There is extreme intersectionality. I haven't really had to deal with a ton of intersectionality, since I'm a white male. Being a white male is, no pun intended, a trump card. You can probably get away with more, in terms of being LGBTQ+ or with a certain religious belief; unless you choose to reveal it, people won't know.

I always had a strong litmus test: Do you accept me or not? Because I don't give a f*ck what people think about me. I've always felt that way. There was a pretty girl in my elementary school in fourth or fifth grade. She was poor—like, Section 8 poor. I remember thinking it didn't make sense that she wasn't hanging with the popular cheerleading types, and it was clearly because she was poor. I remember being young and thinking how stupid a reason that was to not like someone. The fact they were excluding her just because she was poor was dumb. I just learned at an early age that people used arbitrary reasons to exclude people from groups or cliques. I grew up in a very white suburb of Sacramento [California], and I also noticed who was different in a group, because those were the people I always gravitated toward.

My childhood completely informs the way I teach bias training. The precursor to talking about bias is thinking about a group that is pure on the planet. And we all have bias, but we have intraracial issues to work out, too. Like, white people need to have a talk with white people. So, how do you handle those issues prior to handling external issues?

There is a notion of being self-centered and centering yourself in everything. People have gotten to the point where they center themselves about everything. Like, if there is a shooting, someone finds a way to bring up how they were in that same bar or on that street six years ago, and it could've been them. This isn't about you! Everything isn't about you! You have to be willing to solve for misogyny, homophobia, and racism, and have it not be about you or you getting credit for it.

When I teach diversity trainings, I know this isn't my rally, my learning opportunity, or about me. I don't always have to speak. I can listen and learn. In many cases, it is completely counterproductive to be the center of everything. It's one thing I struggle with in regard to affinity groups and employee resource groups.

It seems that if you're part of a certain group, you are automatically "something." It implies you are automatically at more risk or at a deficit. Groups can create a false sense of allyship. I ran the Pride group at Facebook for several years, and the number of straight people who would show up for the party and ride the Pride float and take pictures was huge. But what did you do the other 11 months? People are bragging about canceling their SoulCycle classes and Equinox memberships. But what are your organization's senior leaders' political opinions? Have you asked? If you haven't, you aren't really an ally; you're an opportunist.

This is a token expression or movement, and you just change your Facebook profile filter or header, or use a certain hashtag, or march in a Pride parade and you're done. No, that's not it. This isn't hashtag activism. You are either for something full throttle or not.

I've learned a lot of things about human behavior based on the workplace. First, most people are not organizers, but they will show up—for everything from the Pride parade to theater outings to fundraisers, et cetera. Generally, people need someone to take the lead and they will join, but they aren't instigators. They aren't comfortable, they don't know how, or both. Most people will not go first. The other thing relating to that is people also don't want to hear about a problem; they want a solution. You can get into all kinds of philosophical arguments about whether that's fair or not, but I can't go into many of these rooms and tell people what they can and can't do because I can't be high and mighty about it, and also because it doesn't work. You can't tell some white men they aren't being oppressed. So, instead I think, "How can I be right and effective, instead of right but combative?" There's a time and a place for both.

Diversity training and learning is a job that you'll never finish. You'll have to brace yourself for the duration of what's to come, because it will never finish. In my role as a diversity trainer, the message I try to convey is that your membership in one group doesn't mean you don't contribute to the problem, and secondly, that you still have work to do.

I've gotten to the point of leveraging privilege. Financially, I'm in a great spot in a city I love to live in, and so my "I don't give a f*ck" meter is off the charts. So, if you're a client that wants me to water down training to make you comfortable, I can say no, and I'm not going to do that work. I can be an ally unapologetically. I can also be out and be the person who says the things in the room that no one else will say but they want to. If you are capable of being articulate, smart, and to the point, this is your moment, because it's most needed now.

Jana Rich:
The Advantages of Being LGBTQ+

Bärí A. Williams: What's unique about your background? Tell me about yourself.

Jana Rich: I've been the owner of a talent recruitment and placement firm for five years and previously worked in recruiting for search firms.

I'm from a very small town in Maine. I was adopted at age 2 out of foster care, and aware at a very young age that I was gay. I had the first real cognition of it at 3, and at 13, I was in my bathroom crying because I knew this was it, and it wasn't okay. Because I was from a redneck area, in the truest sense of the term, I knew what it would mean. What is also surprising, to me, is I was never romantically involved with men, and that's one of the easiest ways to hide. I had a boyfriend who came with me to school dances, and he lived an hour away, but we never said anything or kissed, and nothing ever happened. He is still a friend to this day, and he saved me from being harassed more so than if I'd been out. But I look back at that and somehow didn't get involved with someone in a way that felt disingenuous, and I'm proud of that.

BAW: How has your gender identity, gender expression, or sexuality affected your journey? What impact did it have on your sense of self as you transitioned through school and into the workplace?

JR: I went to Vassar, which was an amazing, gay-friendly backdrop. I didn't have my first real relationship until junior year of college, and it was cool. Coming out at Vassar was cool, so you felt more celebrated for being your true self, and based on all of that, I've been out professionally my entire career, including right out of college. I put it front and center, and didn't want to take a job if they weren't comfortable with who I am.

That said, everything wasn't always a cakewalk. I spent 12 years at [consulting firm] Russell Reynolds, from 2002 on. There was a conservative guy as CEO. Every two to three years, they hosted this fabulous event in an amazing location with spouses, and it's all fabulousness. It's a beautiful invite that acknowledges spouses and their help in your work, so I thought, "This is the best thing ever!" A woman colleague knew of my excitement and told me, "You realize this is for couples that are married, right?" But I said, "What do you mean? I don't have the legal right to be married, but everyone knows my wife." I spoke to another male colleague, who was pretty high up in the company, and he said, "If there was a straight couple that was unmarried, they wouldn't be invited, either. But stick with me. I may be the next CEO, and I'm going to push for these things." So, I went on the trip. It was one of the worst professional experiences I had, because I had to explain my wife's absence repeatedly, and it made me want to throw up. Two days into that five-day trip, I just got into a cab and went to the airport and came home and didn't tell anyone.

Sure enough, that gentleman who pulled me aside *did* become the next CEO, and he extended same-sex benefits to those of us that were LGBTQ+.

It was important to me to not just be out in my Stanford GSB [Graduate School of Business] being a lesbian. My point is I'm happy to put myself out there.

BAW: What did it feel like to be "the only" in a work environment?

JR: Bottom line is it's lonely—whether at college, business school, or work. There was only one other out lesbian in my grad school class, and then there's the assumption you'll be best friends. Truth is she's lovely, but we had very little in common.

At work, because I was so out and confident about who I was, I attracted supporters. I certainly found a group of allies and supporters, so I didn't feel alone in having support, but I did in terms of lived experience.

BAW: How have your lived experiences and previous work experiences been influential in building your own company culture?

JR: It's like an episode of *Glee* here. It's a bunch of misfits and we all become a pretty amazing thing. Everyone here is either LGBTQ+, a person of color, or a woman. It's a warm and inclusive environment by design, as we want to demonstrate our mission to our candidates and clients. I want to be clear that if a straight white man wanted to join us and is comfortable with our mission, he can join us! But sadly, some don't lean into our mission, or they look at the composition of our team and feel uncomfortable.

In terms of client base, what's been interesting is in the 5.5 years we've been around, there are two reasons to work with us: We know high-growth consumer tech, and we have a deep connection to diverse and inclusive candidates and how to build those teams. The market initially treated that dismissively. It's problematic now—"That diversity thing was strategic of you, and you really caught a wave." I've been working on this for 23 years, and we didn't come onto the scene and embrace this to increase our revenue. We've been successful because the kinds of clients that come to us are going to be aligned with that mission and at least are wanting that to be part of what we're delivering to them.

More diverse populations, or underrepresented populations, are sensitive to approaches that are disingenuous. We have been successful with recruiting candidates because I and this team have been part of these communities, so we walk in with a different level of credibility. So, we know more people in these spaces than competitors, but we also have the ability, willingness, and knowledge base to fight for that talent. I've had to advocate so hard, for example, [to place] a black woman who was leveled by a white man twice [in her previous job], and I knew enough about [the situation], and referenced her one side up the other, to show that assumptions about her were wrong. If you look at leadership and see there are no women of color, it's not so simple to dismiss her experiences, and I understood that. Sometimes you almost put your reputation at risk, or people think you're sensitive or too vocal, but this what it takes to get people in these roles. It's access and advocacy—it's both things.

We really celebrate the victories here. We have a gong that we ring when we place someone, because it's important to celebrate that, because at the end of the day, the client is making the decision to hire, not us. You also have to lift yourself up in the moments when you don't win. You gotta be easy on yourself, because we can't make the decision—we can advocate, present data, and recommend, but we're not in the position to make the hiring decision.

For founders or those considering being founders, the job of a founder is also exhausting because every single time there's the smallest bump in the road, you have to rearticulate that mission and why it matters. The number one thing I say to them: Try to create your own personal advisory board. It should be people outside of your company but who are going through things that you are also experiencing or they've overcome. It's so critical to have people with similar challenges, who really know you, champion you, and have dealt with the same things. You've also gotta refuel your own batteries, because if you don't, you can't keep going or inspire your team. So, don't forget to refuel.

Charlotte Clymer:
Challenges Are Beauty Marks, Not Scars

Bärí A. Williams: What's unique about your background? Tell me about yourself.

Charlotte Clymer: I'm a proud transgender, gay woman from central Texas; white, able-bodied, but have a mental health disability. I'm also a Christian, and overall, I'm someone who experiences one form of oppression being a trans woman, but I have a number of privileges. So, it's complicated. I'm the press secretary at the Human Rights Campaign (HRC).

HRC is an organization that openly, loudly, and proudly advocates for the rights of those in the LGBTQ+ community, seeking to ensure they are safe, secure, and live out loud at work and in their communities without retribution, harm, or retaliation. The organization prioritizes employment protections, voting rights, and family planning.

BAW: How has your gender identity, gender expression, or sexuality affected your journey? What impact did it have on your sense of self as you transitioned through school and into the workplace?

CC: Overall, I've experienced sexism to an extent, and obviously, transphobia. Being in a progressive space, I have to be careful about how I talk about my military background. It's usually in that order. What's interesting about my line of work, because I'm so visible at an LGBTQ+ organization as a trans person, is I get a lot of hate mail from transphobic people and a lot of requests from cishetero people who ask me for information on what it means to be trans. It's lovely that they are reaching out, and it's in good spirit, but it's information they can Google. I have to consider that if these people are ignored, they may be resentful over that and not want to engage or to learn more. It's hard because you want people to understand and to be open to understanding, but you also don't want to do tons of emotional labor for someone else.

Central to being a good ally is doing the labor yourself. Coming out as trans has made me a better ally across the board. I look back at the times when I was in the closet, and I would ask my friends of color very basic questions on racism and white supremacy. That's something I could've learned myself, instead of having them do the labor for me. The labor piece is so critical. There are so many things marginalized people have to worry about around the basic efforts for the movement for equality and ensuring someone is getting that work done.

I came out in a weird era between grad school and starting at HRC. So, I was able to start my first day as Charlotte and not have to explain anything and deal with the blowback. I am very lucky. I made sure HR knew, and they took care of the rest for me. But again, that's HRC, and they are trained and equipped to do that. One advantage I had was not having to worry about coming out at work. But it does get complicated to the extent I have to come out on a daily basis when I talk to a reporter or a colleague in the movement who doesn't know me. They hear on the phone what they perceive as a male voice, and they ask to speak to Charlotte. I say, "I am Charlotte," and then there's an awkward back-and-forth.

I'm very lucky to work at HRC, and my colleagues are incredible. They don't require me to do that labor for them. But there are colleagues in the larger progressive movement who fail to address things or will put a responsibility on me that isn't mine that requires me to step forward and do the labor, which is annoying. If I were working somewhere else, [I may have a different experience]. I have trans friends that work at regular corporations and organizations who get asked over the water cooler to speak to their niece or son that is struggling with gender identity. This also happens at professional conferences. It may not be in my field, but they work on an overlapping issue, and they want me to talk to a friend of a friend's pastor's grandmother.

Training is really important in these situations. My educated guess is if you talk to the "average" trans person, a little bit of effort goes a long way. It doesn't have to be in the form of "call me by the correct pronouns"—instead, make sure I have adequate access to public facilities and I'm protected from discrimination in the workplace. That's it. And it's not a big lift. I love that there are programs that a lot of workplaces have around visibility and trans people that are famous throughout history. That's great, and do more of that if you wish. But day to day, getting misgendered by a colleague can easily be solved if there are trainings for that, like a Trans 101 educational training. Think of it as, "Hey, pronouns are important, even to people who don't think about them on a regular basis. They matter even to cishetero people, and you would be offended if you were misgendered, especially if you're a cishetero man and are called 'she.' So, think of a trans person."

One of the most pervasive myths I hear about trans people is that we want attention. I spent 30 years in the closet trying to be comfortable in the sex I was assigned at birth. Nothing worked. Now, I do as much as I can to blend in and just do my work. I wish more people knew the things the vast majority of trans people do in life to avoid making people uncomfortable. I avoid going to the bathroom in public sometimes because there may be kids and parents in line and they may be uncomfortable. Then there's going to the gym, and recreational sports leagues. We do so much to accommodate the cisgender folks, just to blend in, and so the notion we are seeking attention is just so far from the truth. It is the opposite.

It's amazing how much coming out makes you a better ally. I know that trans people have to come out all the time. We have to negotiate the space for trans people, and we have to always be prepared for the fact that there may *not* be space for us in certain places.

David J. Johns:
LGBTQ+, Black, and *Not* Boxed In

Bärí A. Williams: What's unique about your background? Tell me about yourself.

David J. Johns: I'm from LA and the executive director of the National Black Justice Coalition (NBJC), a civil rights organization dedicated to the empowerment of black LGBTQ+ people, including people living with HIV/AIDS. NBJC's mission is to end racism, homophobia, and LGBTQ+ bias and stigma.

The organization I lead highlights myths around the white LGBTQ+ monolithic experience. Most people tend to think of white gay men when they think of LGBTQ+ people. So, for people who are not members of that experience, our fluidity around gender expression and identification unnerves them. There are spaces where white people get to move and draw sources of power from their identity, which also provides professional resources they can call upon. There are also other spaces where white lesbian women and gay white men are able to move away from the vestiges of discrimination.

Patriarchy allows white women to identify how they need to as best supports them at the time. We have to be more thoughtful about engaging in exercises that aren't beneficial to us. If I walk outside right now, I don't know that someone would attack me because I'm black or because they think I'm a faggot. I've lived most of my life hearing about how things are based upon my color and what my gender is, or how it is perceived, and to conform and present. I very seldom think about my life and what it means outside of that. So, I appreciate and understand how it may be for women.

BAW: How has your gender identity, gender expression, or sexuality affected your journey? What impact did it have on your sense of self as you transitioned through school and into the workplace?

DJJ: My experience was more about navigating being a Columbia graduate and working for Rep. [Charles] Rangel, who was an elder and a founder of the CBC [Congressional Black Caucus] and was the ranking member of the Ways and Means Committee. I wore a shirt and a tie like my colleagues. I wore a jacket when I needed to meet with members on the floor. As it relates to my identity, there was always conversation around my hair. For most of my adult life, my hair was cut short and in waves. And when I got to DC, my hair was long, but I honestly didn't care. I wore my hair long and curly. It's like a sign of disruption. I'm six feet, five inches. I saw my hair as I do now, as a sign of disruption. People told me DC was "political and conservative." I grew up in Inglewood [California], and I didn't watch *The West Wing* and all that. So, it was just me being me. A lot of people suggested I cut my hair, and I refused to do that. To the extent that was a conscious decision, for some, it was disruptive.

Then I worked for late Sen. Ted Kennedy when he chaired the HELP Committee. I operated from positions of power. When people have conversations about identity politics, it is usually about race and sex. I realize I've had privilege to not have to negotiate that space, and yet it is also less about being a black, same-gender-loving, cis man. So, when it came up on [Capitol] Hill, it was much more being able to offer context around theoretical policies to think about certain communities that would be affected.

The time when I realized [people thought] there was no intersection between being black and same-gender-loving or fluid, I was working on the Hill. People would come and talk about black kids and policy, but they spoke as if they were only heterosexual, and with certain examples, with problematic tropes, like we are all from urban metro areas. Then when people would come and speak about LGBTQ+ kids in schools, they spoke as if those kids were only white. Both of those are wrong assumptions, and I wanted to make sure people saw intersectionality.

When I worked in the White House, I further honored that intersectionality by arranging a summit for same-gender-loving, LGBTQ+, and fluid black and brown kids. If we fail to acknowledge them, we are also affecting how they learn, accept themselves, and show up in the world, so that was important to me. That summit was important because many of those kids contemplated, "Do I even go to school at all?" And what is the social consequence of showing up in places when practices or policies tell you to shrink who you are? I understood that. Some of them were also contemplating suicide. While intersectionality is a thing when it comes to acknowledging policies and how they affect people, it applies first to black women. But my work remains a continued thread in showing up in privileged spaces and being disruptive. Being black, being poor, and being bused to a white, wealthy school in Pacific Palisades [in Los Angeles] was the first time I did that. But it continued and shows up in my work.

Leaning into that experience led me to the work that I do now to ensure teachers, school boards, and school systems make space for all of the students that show up in those places. Now it is the crux of my work. I am fully myself, and my work means I get to translate the work. The work is still very much the same. The specific context and language is different and much more precise now, given the place I am in life. Because of the work we are doing now around discrimination and housing and employment, I know there are eight states that don't allow us to speak about, teach, or acknowledge LGBTQ+ rights. There aren't a lot of spaces of protection, and me being who I am . . . the work is difficult, but anything that otherwise exposes white supremacy, antiblackness, and homophobia and transphobia, I'm here to do it. It's always difficult, but necessary.

I am the beneficiary of people who have leveled privilege to hold space and make space for other people. I have always been conscious about cultivating work relationships and credentials that will "level the playing field," as best as I can level it. So, now, I do the same for others.

Micah Rivera:
Out, Proud, Brown Trans Man in Tech

Bärí A. Williams: What's unique about your background? Tell me about yourself.

Micah Rivera: I'm an out, proud, brown trans man and a product designer. Born and raised in San Jose, [California]. My dad is Mexican, and my mom is white—German and Irish.

The first memory I have of crossing the Golden Gate Bridge was when my family's business went under, and we had to move. We were going to a shelter that had room for us in Petaluma. Later, my dad was working night shift at Food 4 Less, but the house had roaches, and we were just trying to figure out how to live. My dad kicked me out freshman year, and he was physically abusive and didn't like that I was gay or struggling with my gender identity. So, I ended up in foster care, and I was figuring out my sexuality.

There is a lot of trauma involved in foster care, and you can encounter foster parents that aren't that good. You are taught to accept your circumstances and feel helpless, and the problem is that you pass that on. Not everyone is trying to fight over scraps, and when I learned that, it was freeing. I realized I didn't have to fight over scraps but the entire meal.

The key to realizing things and being who you are is removing the shame.

BAW: How has your gender identity, gender expression, or sexuality affected your journey? What impact did it have on your sense of self as you transitioned through school and into the workplace?

MR: I've been out since 17, but before that, I spent years as a very masculine dyke. So, I identify as queer, even though now I identify as a passing man person, and I'm with a woman. People assume we are straight.

I decided I wanted to be a designer because I wanted to create. I gave the commencement speech, I was a Guardian Scholar, and I wanted to speak to the kinds of people like me that didn't have a safety net. I wanted to talk to them about not passing on generational ignorance, or poverty, or not having a home.

It's our job as designers and engineers to break the status quo and to challenge traditional notions, particularly around gender. Tech has the ability to code constructs, and it's our responsibility as practitioners to challenge that and to do less harm. Good intentions grow arms and throw stones. "Fake it till you make it" is the American Dream. You take the grandeur off of "manifest destiny" and this is where you end up.

I've lived on both sides: as a masculine-presenting woman and then as a man. But I'm not making three times as much as when I was a presenting as a woman. I was an art director at a company and found out a colleague made $30,000 more than me, and he was more junior than me. Sometimes, it can be a race thing or a gender thing. To some extent, even though I've transitioned and I'm a man, being visibly brown can be the hindrance to that equal pay or equal opportunity, because all men are still not created equal.

We are decolonizing design in the tech space, because it shouldn't just be rich, straight, white people "solving problems," and in some cases, they are creating new ones. They are like, "We're so woke," and they are bastardizing language to make themselves feel more powerful and able. It's like white feminism. Just because you are privileged and the loudest, you shouldn't be dictating the conversation. Think of black trans women. We have lost 17 black trans women this year, and this isn't affecting white women. What is doing good for you, what does that look like for me and benefits my community and doesn't just make me feel better? How are you improving the community through your products and your experience? If you aren't, you should think about that.

I remember losing jobs by asking people to honor my pronouns before I was male passing. A boss once told me that she wouldn't honor my pronouns because my lunch smelled bad. You will do what you can to make yourself as empowered as you can but somehow still have to be subservient to get by; at least I did until I was male passing. It was hard for people to accept me in certain situations because I always presented as either a masculine-looking woman, like a dyke, or I was male passing. It hyperaccelerated my career once I was male passing, and I've only been designing for six years, and now I lead design for a start-up. I hit the pavement graduating at a disadvantage because I was older, and queer, and didn't have as much experience. People told me before that I was difficult, spoke my mind too much, and now that difficulty is seen as "passion," and people look at it as a positive, as opposed to when I was a female-presenting person. Assuming that male privilege was hard.

There is a definite difference. Sexism is real, and it's alive and well. As a nonpassing trans person who was very identifiable as Latino bodied, if I was giving too much advice or too many comments, people would tell me I was too pushy, too bossy, and too aggressive. As a trans person who was more male passing after taking hormone replacement therapy, people saw me as a man. I can't tell you how crazy the difference was. People would tell me how great, strong, and amazing my point of view is. They encouraged my point of view and how I communicated that point of view and how concise it was. As someone who is more male identified, according to the constructs of masculinity, they pass me the mic more, and women tend to be a bit more wary of that sort of style. I learned two main things. One, sexism is super alive and well. Now that I've assumed this male privilege and leveled up a bit, it's my responsibility to look around the room and see who isn't getting airtime, and to give them my airtime. I'm a feminist before anything, and so I'm also going to big-up women. I surprise people, especially men, with this. Because I'm a dude, people just presume that they can say insensitive and exclusive things to me, but I'm like a Trojan horse, and I will always speak up. To me, it's a responsibility to call people out. That means I have to do a lot of unpaid labor at work, and other places, to call people out and make them aware of what they are saying and doing. I look to the women in my work community to help me process and regulate things when I feel terrible about having to call someone out.

Two, I also didn't want to tell people I was trans at work. Because then they are thinking about your body and not your work or what you bring to the table. Then they want to know if you have had surgery, and how does that "work," and what does it mean, especially if you are partnered. But it does make me more of an ally and allied with those that are people of color, since I am one, and to others that have difficulties or challenges in the workplace. I want people to know you can be all of these things and have meaningful work and a partner, and there are people who will love you. That is what made me be an open trans person and not a stealth one. I want people to know that they can be themselves fully and that I'm in your community and am safe for you to share with and talk to and help you navigate your own journey.

HOW CAN SOMEONE BE
A TRUE ADVOCATE/ALLY?

When it comes to LGBTQ+ rights, there are many ways to be an ally. For example, you can be a mentor who gives advice and observes where it leads the individual you are advising. You can also be a sponsor, which is a step beyond being a mentor. As a sponsor, you bring people into the rooms where decisions are made and showcase their talent. You also talk about the expertise you see in the individuals you are sponsoring, especially during performance and promotion discussions. Finally, you can be an amplifier who ensures that someone gets credit for an idea or action that they initiated. When someone proposes a good idea, you repeat it and give them credit, for example, "I agree with Karen's recommendation for improving our net promoter score," or "I agree with Karen's idea for how to improve our employee participant rate during Black History Month."

Key Takeaways

- Just as *sex* and *gender* are not synonymous, gender expression and sexuality are distinct from one another. For example, a person can receive a "male" sex assignment at birth, be sexually attracted to men, and identify as female. That individual's sexual identity would be heterosexual because the individual is a trans woman attracted to men.

- The importance of pronouns is paramount in the LGBTQ+ community. If you aren't sure how someone likes to be gendered or which pronouns they prefer, ask. It is better to ask respectfully than to misgender someone, which is not only disrespectful but hurtful.

- There is a misconception that because someone in the LGBTQ+ community is out in the workplace, they are open to any and all queries. When it comes to engaging in personal conversations around those matters, follow the leader. People will tell you what they want you to know. If they aren't discussing it, don't ask.

- Provide the space for individuals to make decisions about how they choose to identify and to share those decisions if and when they are ready.

- Some individuals will not and do not disclose their sexual orientation or transgender status because they do not want to distract colleagues from their contributions in the workplace. They do not want to focus on their physical characteristics and instead want people to focus on what they are contributing to the team and the company. If someone is not discussing their status with you, don't bring it up.

PART FOUR

ABILITY AND AGE: UNIQUE CHALLENGES IN THE WORKPLACE

More than 43 million Americans are living with disabilities, which means there's a good chance you will share a workplace with a differently abled coworker. Sometimes differences are readily apparent, as in the case of Tourette's syndrome and mobility issues. Less apparent differences can include addiction, heart disease, hearing impairment, anxiety, and depression, but they require just as much consideration, care, and accommodation as apparent differences.

Age bias is yet another challenge in the workplace. Industries such as banking and healthcare tend to value age, while the technology and entertainment sectors openly cater to young workers. In July 2019, Google settled a class action lawsuit brought by 200-plus former job applicants who alleged they were not hired due to their age. In addition to a payout of roughly $35,000 per plaintiff, the settlement required company training about age bias for employees and managers and the creation of a committee to focus on age diversity in recruiting and to ensure that complaints are adequately investigated.

Douglas King:
Navigating the Challenges of Addiction, Depression, and ADD

Bärí A. Williams: What's unique about your background? Tell me about yourself.

Douglas King: I'm from southern New Jersey, from a town where there's not much there. I'm currently a researcher and programmer but was a sommelier and helped run restaurants. My parents got divorced when I was five. That was very hard, and our grandmother came to live with us—my mother, my grandmother, and my two brothers. Because of the divorce, and because my mother was trying to keep the house, she was always working and my grandmother was the primary caregiver.

BAW: How has age or ability affected your journey? What impact did it have on your sense of self as you transitioned through school and into the workplace?

DK: Early on, had a lot of problems in school. I was capable of doing the work, but for some reason, I would say my main problem was that I was too smart for school. Then I was diagnosed as having ADD [attention deficit disorder] at 17, and I stopped doing some work in school, but I still got by. That enabled me to just coast.

If I wasn't good at something right away, I would stop doing it. I started drinking in fifth grade, and I liked it and would do it about once a month. Then in eighth grade, I decided to stop, and I didn't drink all through high school. That's where the ability to get by just by being good at tests really set in.

My freshman year in college, I was suicidal, and I took an overdose of pills and went to the shower and waited to die. I didn't die, and I told my girlfriend, who told her mother, who told a school administrator, and I had to leave for the semester to get treatment in order to get back in. There, I learned I had depression and was able to get on medication, which I still take. It allowed me to get out of bed, move forward, and know that I could be okay. I returned to school the next semester, I got a job, but I ended up not finishing school because I started drinking more.

After dropping out of school, I told my mom I would be a bartender, and I initially worked at a country club, then a jazz club in Philly, and it was great. I could see great musicians, it was fun, and then I moved to a fancy steakhouse in Philly. There, I became a sommelier. When you are the sommelier, your job is drinking; I make no bones about that, and it gets more progressive.

There was drinking before work, at work, after work; and when you work in a restaurant, it is fine, especially when the boss is drinking. The restaurant owner was also in recovery, and then eventually he started drinking, so it seemed like this was just normal. I also did not get a job because I showed up to an interview drunk. I knew I had the interview, had prepped for it, but I thought I could just have a few drinks to calm my nerves. That ended up with me drinking half a bottle of vodka. I showed up—I'm sure I smelled like liquor—and didn't advance in the process. I laughed about it afterward when I got the notification, but it also made me realize that drinking was costing me opportunities and question what I wanted to do about that, if anything.

I decided to start programming, since I'd done it as a kid. When I realized I needed to transition from the restaurant and wanted to really move into tech and do coding, I decided to take two months off. The idea was that I use the two months from August to October 2012 to train myself to get a programming job. I did not get a programming job at the end of those two months. It took me almost a year to get a part-time job and then a little while longer before I was able to get full-time work. The problem is that I was using those two months to train myself, but I was still drinking. So, I wasn't as effective as I could've been because I was still in the throes of my addiction. At the end of the two months, I was able to work part-time, but February 2013 is when I got sober, and I had interviews during the summer of

2013 and middle of October 2013. I finally got a job working part-time coding. In 2014, I became full-time and stopped working at the restaurant Mother's Day 2014.

I don't feel like I got my life back—I feel like I got a whole new life. If I was just cured of the drinking part, I would've never had to do the hard work of rebuilding relationships and realizing the value of hard work and my contribution to that.

That's the lesson. I wasn't able to make the real changes I needed and do the work I wanted to do until I got sober. I couldn't dedicate the time, the seriousness, or really do the work I wanted without being under the influence. The work environment I was in wasn't conducive to me being healthy, either, and that is something that employers need to be cognizant of. Does your company support and foster healthy activities and ways to bond with coworkers, or does it exacerbate bad habits in the name of bonding?

Then add being bisexual to all of this. Growing up in a small town in New Jersey, there weren't a lot of LGBTQ+ folks there—just a little bit in high school, and then more in college. So, I felt like I never got "Gay 101" or "Bisexual 101." You also deal with hanging out with straight people; they think you're straight. And then when you hang out with gay people, they think you're gay. When drinking, and also being bisexual, I thought monogamy was a trap, and I was limiting myself. What I realized through getting sober was I was always afraid of missing out on things, and so I'd never fully commit because I wanted to keep my options open. That stress also contributed to why I drank.

I pass as straight, so nobody asks any questions, and I don't think about it at times. At work, we started a diversity and inclusion working group in our department, and our retreat was focused on unconscious bias. We were addressing meeting culture, hiring, and retention as a culture, and in that process, I came out to my coworkers as being bisexual. So, although it may not be important to me that this person knows that I'm bisexual, it may be important to speak up so someone else who isn't speaking up knows it is safe.

When I got into tech and felt like I'd learned a bit more, I got involved with Tech Girls. I wanted to give back because I appreciated being raised by two women: my mother and grandmother. When I decided to move into tech, I asked two old coworkers at the restaurant if they had laptops I could use. They did, and gave them to me. They were also two women. So, I reflect on the fact that women are the core of what and who have made me successful.

I'm thankful and lucky to have met people along the way. So, now I pay it forward and give back. When people say they are interested in programming, I give them lists of resources. That's one great thing about Twitter—when you aren't arguing with trolls, when you curate your content and what you're going through—you can find all kinds of resources there, and I like to share them. I made a more concerted effort to follow more women, people of color, and LGBTQ+ folks, and those local to my area. That is more along the lines to diversify my feed and learn more—think globally, think locally.

The interesting thing is that addiction and certain forms of neuro-divergence, like ADD and ADHD [attention deficit hyperactivity disorder], are the last taboos in the workplace. ADD and ADHD are sometimes seen as superpowers. There is this mythology around how you can harness that activity for greater productivity around work, and sometimes you can, if it's managed correctly. But with addiction, it is [one of the only things] around ability that you *can* stigmatize without being seen as judgmental, even though it can be just as harmful, if not more so, than other ailments. It's seen as okay to dismiss because "it's not really a disease but a character flaw." But if you told your employer you had cancer, they would be doing everything they could to help you get well. With addiction, that isn't necessarily the case. Yes, it's a disease, but it can also easily be used as a means to get rid of someone if performance slips or if they are chronically late or sick, even though it's also an ability issue.

Having a workplace that fosters that type of environment and lifestyle [one that recognizes addiction as an ability issue] is key. This is common when I talk to people in other industries, like artists and musicians. There is the fear that you can't relax or even decom-press from work because your usual relaxant isn't there. When I first got sober, I started looking for hobbies to stay busy and be healthy, especially since one workplace had me running around all day and active at the restaurant, and in tech, you sit all day.

The one good thing is there is a lot more focus on addiction and drinking at work now with tech start-ups and ping-pong tables and parties and the #MeToo movement, so there is awareness. People can take away the stigma and also stop plying employees with alcohol.

Libby Leffler Hoaglin:
Age and Gender as Advantages

Bärí A. Williams: What's unique about your background? Tell me about yourself.

Libby Leffler Hoaglin: I'm a former Facebooker, ex-VP at SoFi VP [an online personal finance company], and now at Compass [a real estate tech company]. I've always been in tech. It's an interesting catch-22, being young or presenting as young at work.

BAW: How has age or ability affected your journey? What impact did it have on your sense of self as you transitioned through school and into the workplace?

LLH: I'm very tall, I try to carry myself with a certain kind of composure, and I come across as more mature than I am. I think I present as age ambiguous. I think appearing young does a disservice to someone in the workplace.

I think today you see that catch-22 with women. Are you ready to do the job and experienced enough? And then when you're ready to do the job, people question your age and credentials. The two aren't necessarily linked. Actually, oftentimes they aren't. I had someone ask me during a team transition, "How old are the team members, and how are experienced are they?" My answer to that was, "Let's never talk about that. Let's talk about what everyone is really good at, what they are set up to do well, and how we can help them excel and go further." She immediately asked how many years of experience they had. So, it's the same question, just phrased differently.

Incredible ideas can come from anywhere. They need to be fostered and invested in. The workforce in technology skews younger. So, there is ageism on both sides. For the longest time, it was, "Look at people's résumés and if they hop around, that's a bad sign." Now, not so much. I don't factor that into hiring. People get hired away, and that's okay. The question is if that person has something different or unique to say. Are they like everyone else?

There are two things in the conversation of D&I [diversity and inclusion] that people are starting to talk about but aren't really discussed openly: age and being differently abled. There was not one student at HBS [Harvard Business School] when I was there that was hard of hearing or in a wheelchair. I didn't see anyone in my class that was blind or reading in braille. Where are those people in the mix? All of these things need to be brought into the light to make sure we're working on these problems.

I think "culture fit" is an excuse. I don't think it has any meaning. It is totally ambiguous, and when someone says someone "isn't a fit," what does that mean? Are they capable? Do they have experience? Do they have grit? Are they hardworking and embody the values of what we're doing? You don't have to be a fit to have grit and resilience. I don't want someone who necessarily fits in today. I want someone that will help us get to the culture that we want for tomorrow.

At one company, there was a very smart and successful woman I worked with and respected. She hired for a role on her team and asked me to be on her interview panel. I said, "By the way, there's a great woman on my team that would be interested in this role, and I'm supportive of that." The woman immediately said, "I don't know that she's a fit, or right for this job." I asked why, as I'm her manager, she's kicking ass, she got top performance reviews, and her colleagues love her. This woman, the hiring manager, brought in a slew of candidates, and in the final round they are all carbon copies of her, even down to the look. Did you look at the unconscious bias in that? Are you looking for a fit, or someone who fits in with *you*? Then I had to question why the recruiter didn't flag this or why no one pushed back. She told me she didn't want the woman on my team because she was too junior, but then she hired a woman more junior than the woman on my team.

People use this vague term, "fit," as an excuse. It isn't quantitative; it's very subjective. We need to be thinking about composition of our teams, not just in terms of demographics, but skill sets, and not writing job requisitions that inherently discount certain candidates. This is why inclusion matters most. C-suite sets the tone for that.

So, this is why you don't tell people you want to hire a certain type of person for a tokenism-based reason. Also, you should never say to someone, "Hey, we want you on this panel because we want the perspective of a woman." No, you don't need a f*cking woman! You need qualified and capable people. It's the same thing with age. There's this push and pull with, "You're not qualified; you are overqualified." Then it's, "Well, you don't have enough experience because you haven't been working long enough." We need to be looking at these things in a more blind perspective to give everyone a fair shake to meet their potential.

What people should ask instead of "How old are they?" is, what are each person's strengths? Who are the team rock stars, and who is struggling? What resources do they need? Sometimes, employers are just focused on the "right" thing, and that exacerbates bad results.

Adrienne Lawrence:
The Hidden Superpower of the Spectrum

Bärí A. Williams: What's unique about your background? Tell me about yourself.

Adrienne Lawrence: I'm on the [autism] spectrum, and I'm a lawyer. Being on the spectrum was great when I practiced law because it's a rule-oriented profession. Also, because I practiced at major law firms where the standards of conduct arguably were higher and the expectations were, as well, there was less divergence from the rules, given how much there was to lose. We watched out for one another, recognizing that there are moments of weakness and the stakes are too high to compromise. It was wonderful. My issue, however, was an inability to balance my life with the practice. Because I follow rules, I follow them to a T, not knowing how to pull back on the intensity, giving my all.

Additionally, practicing law was ideal for me because lawyers shot straight—there was no bullsh*t. We were billing clients at $495 to $1,200 an hour, so ego stroking was minimal. That means I got clear and concise directions without any nonsense. And if there was an issue, I got clear and concise feedback. That is very different from other professions where time is less costly.

BAW: How has age or ability affected your journey? What impact did it have on your sense of self as you transitioned through school and into the workplace?

AL: Working in sports broadcast was not conducive to being on the spectrum largely because of the personalities of many of the people. Given that the profession is largely dictated by performance and looks—two very arbitrary and subjective qualifiers that leave one vulnerable to replacement at any time—it can make those working in the industry insecure. As a result, people may do all sorts of things to get ahead and to stay ahead. These are unfortunate aspects of the profession, but they're real.

Being on the spectrum also makes my world appear in black and white. I make fewer assumptions and ask more questions. That means I'm open to more possibilities. This is good and bad. In the legal and broadcast world, it makes me very valuable because I can see things others can't see, as my mind doesn't start with certain assumptions and biases. At the same time, I am vulnerable to bad people. Given that sexual harassment is a problem in some workplaces, in those environments, I am at risk because I'm more likely to take people at face value and to believe them. In law, that wasn't a problem because people were pretty decent. In broadcast, however, because it's a profession based on looks and where women are easily interchangeable, it's a dangerous place to be for someone on the spectrum.

Moreover, I'd say being on the spectrum makes me more secure as a person because I see myself honestly and appreciate my gifts and limitations. Also, if there is a deficiency in me, I learn how to be better and work at eliminating that deficiency. It's checkers, not chess. The law was conducive to my personality because people in law are pretty secure in their abilities and knowledge, given that the law empowers you and your talents are based on your individual intellect and skills. That security is not necessarily something that transfers to other professions.

Galen Pallas:
Ability as Strength

Bärí A. Williams: What's unique about your background? Tell me about yourself.

Galen Pallas: I'm an Oakland [California] native, and I lead partnerships and sales for a tech company. I also have Tourette's syndrome.

Tourette's is a neurodisorder. No one really knows what it is or how it works. But when you want to move your arm, your body provides the right amount of dopamine and energy. My body is constantly producing the neurotransmitters, including dopamine. It builds up and goes to my central nervous system, and so I twitch. I've been told by neurologists and pain specialists I have the most violent version of Tourette's. The good thing is that dopamine also makes you happy, so I'm constantly in a good mood. So, I have patience and tolerance for people's bullsh*t, I hold my temper, and am even-keeled.

BAW: How has age or ability affected your journey? What impact did it have on your sense of self as you transitioned through school and into the workplace?

GP: As an outside sales rep, my job is to call people out of the blue and show up without them knowing me and develop a relationship. And, I chose to sit in the front row in my college classes. I actively choose to contribute in any professional environment I walk into, and feel like I have something to prove versus a "normal" person, so I work harder and smarter and get it done. That also has left employers with the impression that everyone else has no excuse when they don't hit their goals but I do.

In my first sales job, it was a very "tech bro" atmosphere, so everyone always had something to say or had a reaction. So, what I learned to do was to make sure I had something intelligent to say. I started my first job at a start-up when I was 15, so for the most part, when I communicate with customers for the first time, I always address [having Tourette's], because they could misconstrue this as being nervous, or I'm on drugs, or something else is wrong with my performance. Yes, it's a physical disability, but the positive things it's done for me far outweigh those.

It is hard to be vulnerable with strangers, particularly about business, but when I shared, they also shared personal struggles. It allowed me to have hard conversations, not just with customers, but also with coworkers who were also diverse, and about what would be typically inappropriate—what it's like to be black, or lesbian, or of a marginalized religion. It was easy to connect with other diverse and different people, because they also had an interest in learning about me.

That said, I've also heard, "We don't think our clients would feel comfortable meeting with someone like you," so I've been passed on for jobs. Potential employers have also asked, once I've made it to an interview, "Why didn't you tell us on the phone screen that you have Tourette's, or put that on your résumé?" It's an immutable characteristic, and I shouldn't have to reveal anything that I don't want to. I've faced discrimination—people who snicker and make jokes to other people on my sales team who attribute my success to people feeling sorry for me. It is a way to diminish my accomplishments, outcomes, and strategies that I'm good at; and people want to reduce me to this one immutable characteristic.

However, being a straight, tall, white guy, I haven't had to deal with fighting for civil rights in a way others have. So, I know if I fill out the EEOC [Equal Employment Opportunity Commission] questionnaire at the end of a job application and note that I'm a white male, I get callbacks. If I fill out the disability box, I very rarely get callbacks. One superpower with Tourette's is that you can see pattern recognition clearly, so it only took a few times to notice that and understand how to navigate that for the end results I want. I also straddle having a certain set of privileges but also am part of a group that is discriminated against. There have been meetings I've walked in to, and when I start to twitch, people have shown outward disgust and even a feeling of betrayal.

There's been a shift in attitude from my first job in college selling business-to-business office supplies. People thought I didn't belong because I was an Other. They wanted the opportunity I had but used that against me as a reason, saying I couldn't do trainings because I was distracting and that I would turn clients off. In 2008, I took a job selling restaurant and refrigeration supplies. I was dealing with a lot of people that didn't have college educations, and I was selling in rural areas. The familiarity people felt to make jokes and be aggressive in those situations was large. I've had to develop the patience in the workplace to deal with aggression or even basic mistakes. Being a kid with Tourette's syndrome helped me develop thick skin about that because you're used to the questions.

Dealing with certain demographics and in certain areas, particularly rural areas, it makes you think twice about hotels and waitstaff, because you know you will run into a large contingent of people that will snicker or make jokes.

Now, I work for the most diverse and inclusive company I've ever worked for as an enterprise sales rep. I'm responsible for bringing in big customers. I had spinal fusion surgery two years ago, so I'm actually physically disabled now. But the team of people here at Luma Health proactively offered me wonderful accommodations, and they truly understand I can't control the amount of pain I'm in on a daily basis. The transition to being actually disabled was hard, but now I'm also extremely lucky to do what I love, at an inclusive company, and they accommodate me with proactive benefits—certain hotel stays, flying Economy Plus or first-class, and work-from-home days.

"Othering" people used to be something I saw more often. "She was only hired because she's black," or "She was only promoted because she's a woman," or "He only sells so well because people feel sorry for him." I know that still exists, but I don't see it at my company. I wish I could see more of that [inclusion]. I wish companies understood if you had a little bit of everybody in the room, you will avoid a lot of bad decisions and will make better ones.

I've always turned having Tourette's into a positive. It's allowed me to make an extremely diverse group of friends, to ask questions and learn about others in an appropriate way, and I would much rather be in physical pain this way than not having had my eyes opened to the world around me and be emotionally broken, like I see a lot of straight white guys in the country right now. I'd choose this every time.

Cathy Dinas:
Age Ain't Nothing But a Number

Bärí A. Williams: What's unique about your background? Tell me about yourself.

Cathy Dinas: I was the chief of staff to the founder and CEO of All Turtles, an AI [artificial intelligence] incubator/start-up studio in San Francisco.

When I was at Greylock [a venture capital firm], I was the youngest EA [executive assistant], at 25. Everyone was at least 15 years older than me. It makes a difference in how you're perceived at a company. The group of people on your team are older than you, and they wonder if this is your long-term career path—will you get bored, will you jump ship, are you using this as a springboard to something else? When I initially interviewed at a VC firm, it was for a role to be EA to two partners. One wanted to hire me, and one didn't. One gentleman didn't want to hire me if it meant supporting him, as he wanted a career EA—someone who was content just doing that job and wasn't necessarily looking to learn or grow into another role. The other gentleman wanted me, so I was hired.

BAW: How has age or ability affected your journey? What impact did it have on your sense of self as you transitioned through school and into the workplace?

CD: My age, or my perceived age, has always been something I've been cognizant of. I realized that when I look around in rooms, particularly in decision-making rooms full of older white men, I tend to wonder, "Do people take me seriously? Are they listening to my advice, and can they accept my advice, given I may not have as much experience as them in this space and that the advice may come from lived experiences I've had, a moral standpoint, things I've read?" So, folks can't really read me. Then add to that, I have a youthful personality. That's been an interesting journey.

When I was working in investment banking, most of the bankers were older, and at the time I was 22. Analysts tend to be around that age, but you can't tell because they are mostly guys in suits and ties, and if you're in a support role, especially work that requires more soft skills—people skills—than hard skills, you can get someone who isn't formally educated or can be younger as long as they present professionally. The women had kids, were older, and even support staff had worked with their bankers for a long time.

My experience at Greylock was interesting because I was one of their first few black employees. They have yet to have a black investor, partner, or analyst. When you think of VCs, it's a world full of people who are accredited investors and have money to invest. I had an MBA, and I was coming there as an EA. So, even though I was very educated, I was coming in at the bottom rung. When another black woman was interviewing for a role in a different part of the company, I talked to her and gave her information on what salary she should ask for because they had the money, how to interview, who to seek out to work with, who to avoid, and to tell people she knew me during the interview process. She became an ally and a true friend once she was hired.

We carpooled to work and it was great to have someone to lean on. If she hadn't been there, I wouldn't have lasted as long. It was nice to have someone to brief and recap the day with. We helped each other grow, just by being able to share information and giving each other a heads-up about who she was recruiting, what potential investments the people I supported were looking at, and how we could each leverage that information. She also looked young, and was black, so it was the first time I'd been working with someone who was like me. Because we were seen through this intersectional lens of being black women and young, we were perceived as "cool." So, it could be a double-edged sword. Yes, it's nice that people come to us to understand what is important and pertinent to young people in the market, but also that could be a detriment because it could be seen as that being all we have to offer. In the VC world, particularly as an EA, you have to spend a lot of time with someone. It can be hard when you realize the question your bosses are asking is, "Can I see myself spending a lot of time with this person?" Being a young black woman, the answer isn't usually yes. This is especially likely after the #MeToo age. It is easy to just find and grow people who remind you of yourself, and that's never me in this industry.

I like to have fun at work. I don't like to compartmentalize myself. I think black women are good at navigating those spaces where they show up as themselves, because we're being authentic at all times. This is also problematic, because when they don't like you, it's obvious. My fear of bringing my whole self to work is that people will judge me and not take me seriously. I can be heads-down and analytical, but I can also be fun and the class clown. If you have to spend time there all day, you should enjoy that time, and I want to ensure that people around me enjoy the time. I never left a job where I didn't get that feedback. When people have said they really enjoyed working with me, I believe that.

BAW: It's interesting you mention youth being an issue in being taken seriously in some spaces, because in tech, it's a youth culture, where being perceived as older and not as close to keeping your ears to the streets is a hindrance. How do you square those two ideas?

CD: When it comes to being a peer to colleagues, it's fine, but if I'm hired to be the manager, it's a problem. There is still the perception that authority comes from people who are older, and the work isn't as hands-on but is more strategic and offering guidance. People who are younger want to learn from their managers, but the perception from executive teams seems to be "there should be a gap between what you know and what the other employees know," and that's coded language for age. *Experience* is a coded word for *age*, since people tend to believe you can't have experience without also having advanced age.

That's something that needs to be redefined: What and who is a manager, and what can they offer? A manager can be someone who *is* younger than you and can show you how to do work more efficiently, strategically, coaching and inspiring the people that work for them. People mistake age for lack of executive presence, or they presume that you won't have any. So, it can be a pleasant surprise when they see that you have it, or else they cannot even bother to learn more about you because they presume you don't have it.

WHAT SHOULD I KNOW ABOUT THE DISABILITY EQUALITY INDEX (DEI)?

The DEI ranks employers and workplaces to help those who are differently abled to see how prospective employers address their issues and where they rank among employers in addressing these issues. The DEI is a project of the American Association of People with Disabilities and Disability:IN, an international nonprofit resource for business disability inclusion. This joint venture lobbies for the rights and full inclusion of those who are differently abled.

Key Takeaways

- More than 43 million Americans live with disabilities. Although some disabilities are readily apparent, other debilitating conditions, such as depression, heart disease, and autism, may not be visible. Coworkers with these types of impairments also need and deserve care and concern.

- Addiction is a disease, and those struggling with it should be treated with the same compassion as people living with other serious illnesses.

- Prior to the passing of the Rehabilitation Act of 1973, there were no federal laws in place to protect differently abled workers. This act represents the first time that the differently abled community was recognized as a minority group and treated accordingly.

- The mental health of your coworkers is paramount, though discussing it is often actively avoided. Because their mental health affects their ability to get work done, it can affect your ability to complete tasks, as well.

PART FIVE

RELIGION AND CULTURE: FREEDOM OF EXPRESSION ISN'T ALWAYS FREE

Religious freedom has long been valued in the United States. The First Amendment to the U.S. Constitution states, "Congress shall make no law respecting an establishment of religion or prohibiting the free exercise thereof." This amendment seeks to ensure two things: first, that the government will impose no particular religion, and second, that citizens have the right to practice their religious beliefs.

These protections were extended to the workplace in Title VII of the Civil Rights Act of 1964. This legislation protects workers from discrimination on the basis of religious beliefs, affiliation with organized religion, or seriously held ethical or moral beliefs. The law assures employees that they have the right to practice religious grooming habits and wear religious garb and that reasonable accommodations must be made for observance of religious holidays, including flexible work schedules and work policy modifications.

Like religion, expressions of cultural identity can be controversial in the workplace. People of color and members of certain religions have historically had to be careful about how they present themselves to make sure they are viewed as professional. For Orthodox Jews, blending in may mean not wearing a kippah (yarmulke). For black women, it can result in hair straightening or refraining from wearing styles such as braids or dreadlocks. There has been a cultural shift among black women embracing their natural hair texture, and in July 2019, both New York and California enacted legislation called the CROWN Act to protect against workplace discrimination on the basis of hair styles associated with race. In introducing the bill, California State Senator Holly J. Mitchell asked, "Where is the justice when black men and women are denied access to economic advancement because of their natural appearance?"

Jon Park:
When You're More Than Meets the Eye

Bärí A. Williams: What's unique about your background? Tell me about yourself.

Jon Park: I'm head of strategic product partnerships for North America at Facebook, and prior to that I also worked at two other tech companies. I've spent the majority of my career in the tech sector.

I would describe myself as "looks can be deceiving." People in general have natural biases, and rightfully so, based on how they are raised and what they have seen. I do a mental calculation on what people see and take me for before deciding to open up, because I feel as though my bio can quickly become a trivia answer. I ask, "Does this person want to get to know me, or is this a self-serving practice?"

The other part is that I find people say, "Who is this guy, and what is he about?" But what I realize is I want to be known as a father first— father and husband. While there's a lot more to unpack about who I am, if I am not identified as that first, the rest doesn't mean much.

BAW: How has religion or culture affected your journey? What impact did it have on your sense of self as you transitioned through school and into the workplace?

JP: I always grew up knowing I was an Other. As the son of Christian missionaries, understanding and navigating culture was always a norm. Having spent my very early childhood (and subsequent summers later on) in the U.S., I had an affinity for American culture. As I grew older, although fully recognizing my family's culture of origin, I felt a particular cultural affinity toward black culture. There are a lot of different ways to unpack that.

My parents were the first Korean Christian missionaries to land in Moscow after the fall of the Soviet Union. The Korean missionary community is what my family is most tied to. My parents were outliers, especially for their generation. They were both born and raised in South Korea but received their secondary educations and missionary training both in Korea and in the U.S. So early on, they also embraced the feeling of Otherness—when living in the U.S. while studying at an American seminary and in the field among their cohorts who came from a monocultural background.

Throughout my childhood, I didn't feel my full Korean-ness, mainly because my parents sent to me to the main international school, where, although the school name Anglo-American School of Moscow would not lead you to believe it, I was surrounded by a diverse international community. I was surrounded by a bunch of kids whose parents were there for career acceleration opportunities. At the time, in the early 1990s, post-Soviet-era Moscow was chaotic, and being a part of a landing team for a multinational corporation or being a foreign service member for your government was a catalyst and career-defining stepping-stone. To help families adjust to the chaotic surroundings, the international school was basically a perk for families relocating—a haven that provided safety, security, and privileged opportunities to the enrolled students. Those were basically, at a high level, the premise of a lot of why my family's friends were there.

I felt really comfortable being an Other because of the communities I grew up in. Although people tried [to understand me], I didn't ever feel fully heard or seen. There were parts of my life that even the other Korean students wouldn't fully get. As the only Asian American kid in my school, I grew up subconsciously and consciously aware of my Otherness. So, I became comfortable with the fact that no one may fully get me.

Throughout my school experience, I felt my Otherness in multiple facets—both culturally and socioeconomically. Due to the demographic breakdown of the school, most of my friends were

Americans—they were Caucasian—or from another country. Aside from myself and a couple of Latinx classmates, there weren't any "hyphenated" people in my network throughout my childhood—no African Americans, Asian Americans, et cetera. Instead, they were kids who self-identified as Korean, Swedish, Dutch, American, Zimbabwean, South African, Pakistani, et cetera. As the only Asian kid who felt more American than Asian—yet also not fully embraced as being truly American, either—I was constantly reminded of my Otherness. I can't count the number of times I had to navigate around the "Where are you *really* from?" question. My parents also being the only ones who weren't involved in foreign service or corporate-sector work also created the feeling of Otherness. I spent weekdays in my school bubble, but was constantly exposed to the underserved, underprivileged, and abandoned communities that my parents were called to serve. Their ministry included supporting pensioners, people in mental institutions, orphans, and the homeless. Juxtaposing traveling to cities like Prague and Vienna for school sports tournaments with serving at my parents' soup kitchen, I was acutely aware that life isn't always about the work you put in. As a kid, I realized that socioeconomic inequality and being poor or having less than others is often based on circumstances beyond people's control, and not because "you deserve it."

As an elementary school student, I became obsessed with biographies. My weekend reading led to me learning about the African American experience, specifically starting with Dr. King and the civil rights movement. Learning more about an entire community that was systematically oppressed due to their Otherness was something that drew me in. Learning more about the 1950s and 1960s took me down a cultural immersion path and led me to the music, starting with Motown—that's where my love for good music started. From there, I got into hip-hop, R&B, and soul music. And my love for the music and the culture carried me through my middle school and high school years.

During the college application process, I wanted to apply to schools that satisfied a few needs—namely, a traditional campus experience, one where I could operate freely as an Other, and one where I would be challenged outside of my comfort zone. I looked at schools with fairly low Asian populations when I assessed the schools I got into. I thought about how I could operate as an Other and not one of many. I would have felt pressured to be involved with certain communities, and that would stifle me. I have an intense need to be understood, but I was worried that the communities I thought would understand me would only understand at the surface level. I wound up choosing the University of North Carolina at Chapel Hill for that reason. It satisfied the longings I had for a traditional campus experience, a small-enough Asian population where I wouldn't feel pressured to "fit in," and a new experience in a part of the U.S. that I never experienced. At Carolina, I was able to thrive by being a member of the only black a cappella group on campus throughout my four years—shout-out to Harmonyx—and being a member of the Black Student Movement while also finding ways to connect with the Asian American community without feeling like I had to fit into a mold.

BAW: How has your unique cultural experience affected you in the workplace?

JP: For one, tech is predominantly white and Asian men, and that privilege isn't lost on me. Having to navigate different countries, languages, and what feels like different worlds has been a benefit. It has afforded me the ability to blend into different environments as needed, and it hasn't been as taxing. But I don't know that I would be able to say that and do it if it weren't for growing up as a Korean missionary's kid in a foreign country with a different language. That experience has helped me to move through workplaces easily and to learn to adapt on a dime with little or no information. That also is an advantage in tech, because things can change so quickly.

Because I've always operated as an Other in every space I've been in, I start off by assuming everyone has their own story or journey. Those are surface-level data points, but that's at least how I try to be approachable and as vulnerable as possible to someone. So, guaranteed, I will never run into someone who is able to guess my background. I'm okay with that, because I know I won't be accepted based on my background or my education.

Everyone has a story, and I appreciate that story. It even makes me more tolerant of people that may be difficult to work with or if the way they work is difficult. I play devil's advocate for some, but that's because I want to understand and give the benefit of the doubt that their energy and journey aren't what I would expect or understand.

And as I gained more experience, I would ask myself, "How do I share my journey with people when I see there is opportunity for them to benefit from that, as well?" In general, I try to take a little more time and not treat interactions like a transaction; I don't want to treat people by their output. If things are so black and white that you only value what someone produces, and not the context in which they are struggling in their production or why they are doing so well, it minimizes the person but also feeds into biases.

It took me some time to accept the fact that my Otherness is not a weakness or deficiency. I realize that my superpowers are care and context, and in reality, my experiences and ability to navigate different environments while fully embracing my Otherness are my greatest assets and strengths.

I've seen every opportunity I have as a gift, and for any or no reason, and I was fortunate that these things happened to me. That is the underlying motivation for me. I know that these opportunities don't come to everyone, so I can't approach it as if they come to everyone or will come around again. There are no guarantees. For that, I need to be a better steward.

Amy O. Hampton:
Wine, Christianity, and Entrepreneurship

Bärí A. Williams: What's unique about your background? Tell me about yourself.

Amy O. Hampton: I'm an entrepreneur and wine connoisseur. I was a hospital executive, and I remember being in a boardroom and feeling like it wasn't for me. So, I started making my own wine cocktails at home. I would look at people, note what they liked, what seemed to tickle taste buds, and then I'd go to Whole Foods and get ingredients and thought of what I should do, and just go make it at home and try it out.

BAW: How has religion or culture affected your journey? What impact did it have on your sense of self as you transitioned through school and into the workplace?

AOH: I was raised in a house with tradition, and I woke up one day and decided to buck that to an extent. When you are raised with [a traditional upbringing], you have to grow out of that and learn how to deal with it. I was on the way to being president of a hospital, and that is what I was focused on, until someone said I should think about doing [my wine cocktails] full-time. So, I decided to do that.

The way I spelled my wine, Sociologie, is a love letter to women. I wanted something to express sociology as a study, but it's also a way to have fun while studying what people like and want, and show it in a different prism. I wanted to make sure women knew the options around them, from that standpoint.

The dichotomy of life is trying to figure out your flow, and what you need to do, and how to manage all of it. That's the miracle part of being an entrepreneur, to step out of being fearful and still be on point.

When you find you are a butterfly, you can't kick it with caterpillars anymore. When you go through that metamorphosis, your mind doesn't work the same way anymore. You can't relate. So, you have to choose, and that isn't a bad thing. I choose to be a butterfly.

BAW: Let's explore more around your Christianity being a visible and vocal part of who you are. You are a classic Southern belle, God-fearing and open about it. How does this affect how people see you in the wine and spirits industry? And how do you navigate that?

AOH: Well, it's sometimes a justified juxtaposition. It's like a constant duality of being pressed, and that your life *is* water to wine. It doesn't have to be one or the other. You almost always have to be affirmed that it's okay to be juxtaposed between these two worlds, of secular and Christian. I get more judgment from the Christian community than I do from the wine and spirits industry [because of] the whole idea of, "It's the devil's juice. It's his elixir." But those are the same people who are asking me to send them a case of wine or have their assistants come pick up wine so they aren't seen, or they'll have someone else pay for it so it won't be tracked back to them. Now, *that* is funny.

Being in the wine and spirits business, there are things that don't align to Christianity. So, in some ways, it is getting to shine a light on how a Christian can be in this business, be responsible, and be about my business. When I'm at events, people often watch me and think, "How are you going to act? What are you going to do?" So, what I do is demonstrate the love of God and celebratory spirit, and I share of myself, my wine, and community.

Wine is even a demonstration of the miracles of Jesus. Grapes don't spoil when they are pressed—they turn into something greater under pressure. Why be regular? Why live a regular, boring life? It is an example of being yoke free—it's like having the essence of being light. It's not about being drunk but to let loose and celebrate life. You can be loose without being lost. You can be sober in mind, have some wine, break bread, and love life with one another. It doesn't have to be one or the other. It is also demonstrating fellowship and communion, and even communion has wine! So, I don't see how there is a hypocrisy in what I do, though sometimes others do and question it. It's about love and light and celebration, not being inebriated.

A lot of times people look at Christianity and think it's easily boxed in and also judgmental. I'm here to serve as an example that that isn't true. That's the gospel itself: There is no judgment. It's all glory. That's also why I'm here: to serve as an example that someone like me can be in this business, because you can call on more people when they see me having a good time. Christianity is also about having a good time— why worship a God that makes you feel bad? I can serve as an example of *not* being that way by showing my personality, my God-given spirit, and by sharing my wine. The larger thing is my business itself is an example of my Christianity, because my business was a complete leap of faith, and I'm faithful, and grateful, every day.

Manik Rathee:
Religion, Race, and Influencing Assimilation

Bärí A. Williams: What's unique about your background? Tell me about yourself.

Manik Rathee: I work in tech and enjoy being a product designer and UX [user experience] engineer. I'm Indian, and my parents are Hindu. My name is based on Sanskrit, and it's tricky to say because the Hindu language can be hard. The *a* is like a *u*, and like you rolled the *n* into an *r*. I tend to just let people use the pronunciation "Manic," though it is "Mon-ik," like "Monday" but with an "ik" at the end. That's probably the first concession that I've given in the workplace. I started to think about that as I thought about religion and the workplace: Did I default to the easiest and most relatable mispronunciation of my name for ease and time saving, or for the comfort of the person I was talking to?

Now I focus on building good, inclusive products. I was at a small advertising agency in New Jersey, so I got to do some copywriting, some design, and then responsive design, which was a crucial part of my career. From the agency work, I continued to freelance, and then moved to the Obama campaign to do UX engineering with the donation platform, and it was the first responsive platform campaign ever. Of course, I did this with a team and was by no means the main and only contributor.

From there, I worked with Nest, and now I'm at Google and work closely with design teams. I want to remove any friction and walls between those teams. The way to create inclusive products is to remove barriers between the two. I am also working on a diversity-and-equity initiative to drive a proactive approach to make sure products are inclusive.

BAW: How has religion or culture affected your journey? What impact did it have on your sense of self as you transitioned through school and into the workplace?

MR: As early as first grade, I could remember standing out as an immigrant, and later, because of my religion. I went to public school in a predominantly white and Christian area, and they weren't very diverse. There were one or two Indian kids I knew, and they felt the same way. We stood out like a sore thumb. There's generally a lack of knowledge and awareness of what it's like to be Indian or clarity of what it means to be a Hindu. That, obviously, became a sticking point for a lot of those kids.

Initially, I didn't think that affected me. I knew who I was and how things worked. And I am a firm believer in science, because there is a great sense of logic involved in science, but there are things that are unexplained, and I still believe in the tenets. Maybe there is this other being or other energy or force that is there.

For my parents, as immigrants, religion was a big part of their lives. There was immersive learning and a class to read and write Hindi taught by the head of the mandir [temple]. My race is tricky because

I'm a light-skinned Indian, and during summer, when I tanned, people would assume I was Spanish. Other people thought I was Greek, so that was tricky to deal with, as well, because I could sometimes get around the immediate knee-jerk kid reaction to race. In other cases, people knew it and would lean into it because I didn't look as "different" as they thought I should.

As I was in elementary school, we had a cultural show-and-tell. I was in fourth grade, and we had the chance to exhibit how we make cultural decisions differently, et cetera. I brought in my notebook from school at the mandir [Hindu temple]. There were bright Sharpie colors of different religious symbols, and there was the swastik, which is now known as the swastika due to the language. My teacher took me outside and told me to cover it up, and that she had electrical tape to cover it, because it was offensive and affiliated with being a Nazi. The nuanced detail is this was part of the religion—not just Hinduism but several other ancient religions—as a common symbol that means "prosperity." It reflects the sun and source of energy and prosperity. But it was co-opted by the Nazi regime, and they clumsily removed the four circles and tipped it onto the corner. So, this was one moment, and 30 seconds of a conversation with an authority figure in my life, and I never drew this symbol again. I had kind of separated myself from it due to that moment. Didn't realize it then, or in high school and college—around the same time I stopped correcting my name. The message I received as a young child was, "Your religion is offensive. The things it's made up of will make these white people unsettled, and we need to make sure they are comfortable." If I have to suppress entire parts of myself for others' comfort, white-centric society is very tied to white supremacy, it's a step away from systems of white supremacy today. That one step can't be removed entirely, it may not be in bad faith, and people may not be active white supremacists, but they are complicit, and I am complicit, as well, by catering to them.

The balance of race and religion was tricky for me, and growing up with that was a challenge. I didn't know how much of it I should express. [Openly expressing my religion and culture] brought extra attention, or someone would bring it up, so I stopped and focused on *not* doing it and, instead, "fitting in." When my parents came to school events, how did they fit in? They had accents, and would people mock them? They could deal with it, but that was a different thing for me to deal with that I don't think I ever reckoned with.

The older I got, I saw it wasn't that big of a deal. The diversity increased in each place and step, and the racial balance in Newark [New Jersey], where I went to college had a lot of everything: poverty, minorities, some well-to-do areas, and in between. This was a culture shock because I was raised in a primarily white, well-to-do area, and this was a new scene that was predominantly black, brown, and Asian. I was invisible in a positive way. I could go about work and about my way without thinking about it.

Moving through college, I thought a bit more about race and religion because of societal structure that exists, and I wasn't taught that in high school and middle school. I took a class on recidivism, and that was unbelievably eye-opening to me. I didn't know the concept of the school-to-prison pipeline or what happens upon reentry to the population. I realized I was raised to respect authority blindly, not with context or reactions, but to do what they say. I didn't question it.

As I got more into this work, I realized it was a lot easier for me to do a project or read about these issues than to get my hands dirty. So, at work, I just looked at it as my first real job and that I should put all of my effort into it. That logic was fine, but it's not either/or. I had to understand how that energy was going to be spent and how I was going to maintain it. I knew it would be a lifelong journey to understand these topics, but I also wasn't afraid to do the work to learn and accept it.

My role with the Obama campaign brought some of the most formative and impactful moments of my life. The reason for that is exposure. I was in headquarters in Chicago on the engineering team. The team had such radically different experiences. They were from all over the country, they had different lived experiences, and I realized I hadn't met anyone that was [out] in the LGBTQ+ community. Through my own experiences of lack of understanding or knowing cues, I hadn't been exposed to this. And this was radically different on the campaign, because everyone was very open about who they were.

What I went through as a light-skinned Indian Hindu man in a pre-dominantly white area was incredibly different and trivial as opposed to what others went through. When I compare my lived experience to many other groups, it was a mild inconvenience that I could overcome, versus lifelong limitations certain groups have that they can't overcome. Or, if they overcome one, there is another one waiting for them.

What I learned in this work environment was the impactful use of language—how doing or saying something without malice still didn't negate the impact or hurtful nature of the words. For instance, saying something was "girly" may not be malicious, but there is power behind that. For someone who looks white saying that, and someone who is male saying that, there is power behind that, and I didn't know. I had to learn and reassess my gut responses to things, how I received things from other people, the words they use or don't use, and it was an extension of the learning I had in college. There was a reason to be killing ourselves to [work in the campaign]—with unhealthy hours, not the best meals, et cetera.

Working at bigger companies, you have to work against the tide [in order to] change. You have to call out larger things and go from there. As a lighter-skinned person, I can talk about things in a manner other marginalized people can't. I leaned into that quite a bit during the campaign, and every moment afterward. I don't have to deal with the impact that another person of color who brought that up would. That's a power, or strength: I can deal with my own reaction to it, and not internalize it, then use it to further the goal. This is something that could actually change who can use a product and who is included in the discussion to begin with.

This was paired with my own internal growth. I learned what people had to go through in order to gain their rights and access, and I think now it's less of a struggle to challenge other viewpoints; it's becoming more of a habit, which is crucial for me. That means I'm still growing and putting in the effort, which is the key part that's required to con-tinue to grow and make an impact wherever possible.

A newer learning for me is whether I'm centering the right things for myself, and for people of color generally, and dealing with it in real time. It's building the muscle to talk about race and religion, what's the accepted version, what would happen if I use an improper term—not a negative term, but what doesn't seem correct—all of those little building blocks helped me with viewpoint challenge and growth.

The choices that I made all the way back in elementary school until now—how would they be different if I knew then what I know now? Thinking of those instances—how they affected my personality, and is that something I would've chosen to do on my own? This growth is new to me, and is what I've been doing the last three to four years. Sometimes, I still optimize for the comfort of other people so we don't spend five minutes talking about how to pronounce my name.

Does my religion or race facilitate me continuing to be a better person or act in a better, positive manner to effect change? I think that either direction will help me get there. That's where all of these life experiences have gotten me today. For myself, this is a much more conscious question. It's much more in my face now. If I talk about the struggle of being Indian, someone else speaks on being a black woman, or someone talks about being an Indigenous person who is also trans, they will be inundated with hate, and that's not conducive to growth.

Samara Rivers:
Transforming the Spirits Industry as a Black, Christian Woman

Bärí A. Williams: What's unique about your background? Tell me about yourself.

Samara Rivers: I'm from LA, and above all things, I'm a mother of two small kids. I'm someone who is passionate and determined to do good in this world, and the way I choose to do that is through the spirits industry. That's the way I've decided to leave an impression and make an impression in an industry that has been untapped, though one of the oldest industries in this country, it could really use some modern-day finesse and new blood.

BAW: How has religion or culture affected your journey? What impact did it have on your sense of self as you transitioned through school and into the workplace?

SR: I came into this as a lover of fine spirits with a background in event planning and nonprofit administration. I came to this industry as a consumer. I met someone who needed assistance in planning events, and I basically got a subcontract based on someone not knowing the bars and events in the Bay Area. In doing that, in meeting the client obligations, I realized there was no direct consumer marketing [geared toward people of color] in the whiskey and bourbon industry. I found a hole and decided to fill it.

BAW: How do you reconcile being a Christian in the spirits industry when many Christians harbor negative judgments about those who drink?

SR: To be clear, I don't drink all the time or every day. My main goal is to influence how the spirits industry reaches and markets to consumers of color, and also to see people of color ascend within these spirits companies. Those are very "sober" conversations, and you have to be fully cognizant and present for those conversations.

The industry leans into its own stereotype. They have white men with low buzz cuts, tattoo sleeves, handlebar mustaches, and they are very "hipster" white guys. That's the description of the average brand ambassador for spirits companies. But BBS [Black Bourbon Society] is speaking up, women are speaking up. We aren't going to allow this and instead ask, "Why can't I be the brand ambassador for this? Why can't we show we are part of the brand and how you approach us?"

I walked into a meeting with a white woman brand rep, and her response was, "I didn't know that black people drink bourbon." So, even when someone should appear to be an ally, it was information that wasn't incorporated as a target for her or something that she should even consider. She and I are now really good friends, and she sees the 9,000 members that BBS has, but the industry had no idea we existed and she was an example of it.

Because of that perception, I was able to make an impression quickly. Sometimes being a woman and being a woman of color is an advantage, because the standards are so low.

Companies aren't loyal to women of color. I spent many hours and late nights grinding for the nonprofits I worked for, only to be told that it wasn't sufficient or I needed to be present more because the place was family-friendly. To be in a toxic work environment is very hard for me, and I feel like that trickles from the top down, particularly for women of color. They say it's eight to five, but if you leave at five, everyone side-eyes you. If I was going to dedicate that much time to an organization and a mission, I would put it into my own and make five times more money. The only person I'm accountable to is myself, and I know I won't let myself fail. When you are your own boss, things are a lot different. It isn't easy. There are a lot of dark days to go along with that. If you are following your purpose and your passion, you will always be okay. And so far, I've always eaten. But whatever I do, I have to be at peace and be happy.

What I've learned from prior experiences, especially as being in two groups [a sorority and a nonprofit group benefiting children], is I'm a lot more forgiving of my staff, and family is always first. The majority of my staff are women, and children come first, and I get it. My publicist is an example. She had cancer when I first hired her and was in chemo. At that time, we had been in the *New York Times* and *Forbes*, and she was pitching me for TV. I wouldn't discount her because she was sick. I was committed to making it work. She said, "I need you to give me a bit of grace," and I did. She clearly doesn't need to be micromanaged, and she manages me. When you empower the people you work with and trust them to do their jobs, you have so much better relationships with them. To give that also affords me grace. Give everyone some grace.

Rabia Chaudry:
Hijab as Power

Bärí A. Williams: What's unique about your background? Tell me about yourself.

Rabia Chaudry: I'm an author, activist, and attorney. I am the public advocate of Adnan Syed, the wrongfully convicted man at the center of the most popular podcast in history, *Serial*, and author of the *New York Times* bestselling book *Adnan's Story*.

BAW: How has religion or culture affected your journey? What impact did it have on your sense of self as you transitioned through school and into the workplace?

RC: My parents immigrated from Pakistan in the 1970s. When my parents naturalized a few years later, I had the privilege of becoming a citizen. I'm the eldest of three, with a younger sister and brother.

Being a U.S. citizen and having that blue passport is such a privilege, and people don't realize that. When you travel and people recognize [a U.S.] passport, it is like a silent stamp of approval, and people treat you differently.

My father was a veterinarian, which was shameful for the family. It was never a conversation—the expectation was to be a doctor—and he ended up being a vet employed by the Department of Agriculture. That led to living in many rural areas. Growing up in a small town with not a lot of people of color, I didn't realize I was an Other until middle school or high school, when people started to point out I was not like them. But I was pretty oblivious to it until then, because I wasn't treated differently, and I had my family.

When I went to college in Baltimore [Maryland], that was the first experience with lots of diversity and a big city. Of course, I was also expected to be a doctor, but I struggled in the sciences and decided

I couldn't take the MCAT and instead took the LSAT and did really well without trying. But I got married in my last year of college, and so by the time I went to law school, I was married with an infant and living with my in-laws. This limited my ability to participate in law school fully, from [working on the] journal to other extracurricular activities.

I was interested in criminal practice but was worried about taking the emotion and burdens of the cases home. I was offered internships at the DC Public Defender's office and an immigration law firm. I wasn't sold on the idea of the immigration firm but decided to give it a try. When finishing that internship, 9/11 happened. During this time, the Department of Homeland Security was created, and Muslim men had to register for national security purposes, and I noticed that they would go to register and didn't come back, and this worried me greatly and gave my work a new purpose. I saw how much it mattered.

In the courtroom, I would not wear the hijab, and judges would still ask where my lawyer was. At that point, I was divorced and a single mom. Then I worked at the Department of Health and Human Services. When a woman wears a hijab, one of two things happen: Either you become invisible—they won't make eye contact—or you are too visible and get negative attention; they stare and make comments. For the most part, I felt like I disappeared, which was hard considering I'm not a wall-flower. Another thing it did for me—the organization was heavily men, so there was a ton of sexual comments and sexual harassment around me, but because I wasn't seen, they weren't as aggressive with me. The behavior was inappropriate, but it was before #MeToo, so it was treated casually. It was just like . . . a thing men did without reproach.

So, when I went back into private practice in immigration, I made a very conscious decision to work with a law firm with clients who were Central and South American. I did so because most Southeast Asian men have a good deal of entitlement and machismo, and I didn't want to deal with it. And in Southeast Asian culture, lawyers are the bottom of the rung in terms of career. The intercultural issues made me want to seek out a different client base, as the disrespectful nature of Southeast Asian culture toward lawyers made me feel I couldn't do my best work—add to that the irony of others within my cultural and religious community demeaning and discrediting my work. There was an Arab couple who I had previously had a consultation with, and they provided a retainer. They later came back and told me that they didn't want to hire me, as they didn't think a judge would respect me because I wear a scarf—and these are other Muslims! They said I was smart, competent, and able to help them, but they were concerned about how I would present, and represent them, in a courtroom. They decided to hire a Jewish male lawyer in the end.

What I realized halfway through my career was, "I have to stop wearing a scarf to get ahead, or I just have to be myself, and people will suck it up and deal with it. I'm going to get stuff done, regardless." Because I'd been doing advocacy work in the Muslim community for years, I was getting called on to do media on TV, panels, and the like. But then it made me think, "Am I the token Muslim with a scarf?" It began to feel like I was making people feel like they were checking a box to make their liberal sensibilities feel good. That said, some doors did open up because I have a scarf on, so I'll show up and show up as good as or better than anyone else. Because of that, when you see a Muslim woman in the future, you will see her as capable, smart, and strong, too.

Post-*Serial*, this has been some of the best time in my career, because I've been allowed the freedom to talk about things that are not just about terrorism, and I can be and look like myself. To be able to work in the wrongful-conviction space is wonderful. I can talk about advocacy, digital media, criminal justice reform, and the intersection of all of those pieces without pause. It's actually welcome.

For my podcast, *Undisclosed*, we investigate wrongful convictions and the U.S. criminal justice system. Podcasting allows people of color to learn about you, your interests, interesting stories and cases, and it isn't reliant upon who you are and immutable traits. Plus, the barrier to entry is low. I don't have to be a six-foot blonde to be on a podcast, as you need certain optics to be on TV.

For *Undisclosed*, we often analyze cases that are based in rural communities. Navigating the dichotomy of being an immigrant Muslim woman with a scarf dealing with cases in rural communities is interesting, as that demographic typically wouldn't be receptive to me or my help, but in this case, they don't care because they want the help and appreciate my skill set.

It's something to negotiate delicately. I find cases via the Innocence Project, and they will send cases to *Undisclosed*. Sometimes lawyers reach out, sometimes families will reach out, and sometimes we find them on our own. I'm currently working on a double-homicide case in backwoods Tennessee, and while investigating the case on site, I put my hair in a bun, wore a baseball cap and jeans, and took my white woman lawyer partner, Susan, to assist. At the end of the day, it's about the case and not your ego. So, if you have to make certain calls to get the work done, you do it. It's about getting justice for someone, and that may mean certain modifications.

I personally don't believe in social and religious isolationism. Social media attacks also come from the Muslim community about my interfaith work. I participated in a fellowship cohort, Shalom Hartman Institute, with other Muslim Americans in conjunction with an Israeli component around the land and shared space of Palestinians and Israelis. People berated our cohort members for participating in this and trying to understand the Jewish community and why the land in Israel is so special to Israelis. The other cohort members were chastised online, and they publicly apologized, disavowed the program, and asked for public penance in order to be accepted into the community. I told them they could boycott me, but I wouldn't boycott them, nor would I just go away. I'm still a part of the community, and they are still my people. Slowly, I've worked my way back into the community in an accepted, meaningful way again.

HOW IMPORTANT ARE AESTHETICS?

Aesthetics are incredibly relevant for every community that was a victim of colonization. Early racial theorists, for example, Christoph Meiners and Johann Blumenbach, declared that those who are "Caucasian" or fell within the category of "white" were the most beautiful race. So, along with the redistribution of resources, colonization brought standards of beauty that were often in direct opposition to the standards of beauty of those colonized. The following are pertinent to every community in which European colonization occurred:

Colorism. A form of primarily intraracial prejudice (prejudice among people of the same race against one another) that privileges light-skinned people of color over dark in areas such as income, education, housing, and the marriage market.

Hair texture/natural hair. Classifying someone on the basis of hair texture is relatively new. Hair that is of a looser curl and of a texture closer to that of a white person, is viewed as more beautiful. Black women with hair classified as 3A or 3B in a widely adopted hair typing system in which hair textures are categorized from 1 (straight) to 4 (kinky or coily) are seen as most desirable.

Accents. The distinctive way someone speaks can be an indicator of their place of origin and is often judged by its aural appeal to the dominant culture. How thick or strong an accent is can also be a socioeconomic marker. For this reason, newscasters ensure they don't have "accents."

Key Takeaways

- Some visual markers are an outward sign of a person's religion. Do not challenge the reasons people wear certain garb.

- Religion is an identifier but not the only one. For some, religion is something that connects them to their family and how they were raised. For others, it is a demonstration of things they want to change.

- Culture is about what people are exposed to and how they incorporate it into their lives. There are formative times during which culture can shape how people view the world.

- It is important to understand the context that shaped your colleagues' formative years. It is also vital to understand and respect the fluidity of culture based on popular culture, race, ethnicity, and even the diction that comes from those influences.

- Religion can be both a unifier and an isolator. Approaching people from a place of curiosity and understanding will advance the cause of the marginalized religious person. In addition, it will help satisfy your desire to understand the beliefs of or influences on colleagues and their world views.

Resources

Books

Christians at Work: Examining the Intersection of Calling and Career by Barna Group
Explores how one finds purpose in professional life and how that purpose aligns with personal beliefs and life.

Overcoming Age Discrimination in Employment: An Essential Guide for Workers, Advocates & Employers by Patricia G. Barnes
Tackles demonstrating value and worth as a marginalized community without representation.

Geek Girl Rising: Inside the Sisterhood Shaking Up Tech by Heather Cabot and Samantha Walravens
Offers an insider's view of what it's like to work in Silicon Valley and provides advice on how to combat gender discrimination.

Better Allies: Everyday Actions to Create Inclusive, Engaging Workplaces, by Karen Catlin
Presents actionable tips on creating a welcoming workplace for the LGBTQ+ community in particular.

Can You Afford to Ignore Me? How to Manage Gender and Cultural Differences at Work by Elisabet Rodriguez Dennehy
Discusses and offers tips on managing gender and sexual harassment in the workplace.

Allies at Work: Creating a Lesbian, Gay, Bisexual and Transgender Inclusive Work Environment by David M. Hall
Presents a guide to creating cultural change in the workplace and developing work environments that fully include everyone, including those on the fluid gender expression and sexuality expression spectrum.

Mental Illness in the Workplace: Psychological Disability Management by Henry G. Harder, Shannon Wagner, and Josh Rash
Presents a study of the effects of psychological disability at work and what employers can do to help their employees.

The Memo: What Women of Color Need to Know to Secure a Seat at the Table by Minda Harts
Offers advice from the perspective of marginalized communities.

Intersectionality by Patricia Hill Collins and Sirma Bilge
Examines how intersectional frameworks speak to topics as diverse as human rights, neoliberalism, immigration, global social protest, and citizenship worldwide.

Crippled Justice: The History of Modern Disability Policy in the Workplace, by Ruth O'Brien
Discusses disability policy in the workplace from World War II to the present.

The Shield of Silence: How Power Perpetuates a Culture of Harassment and Bullying in the Workplace by Lauren Stiller Rikleen
Describes how to deal with the threat and fear of retaliation that prevents people from coming forward with allegations of sexual harassment.

We Can't Talk about That at Work! How to Talk about Race, Religion, Politics, and Other Polarizing Topics by Mary-Frances Winters
Describes how to broach difficult topics at work and deal with the questions that arise.

Generations at Work: Managing the Clash of Boomers, Gen Xers, and Gen Yers in the Workplace by Ron Zemke, Claire Raines, and Bob Filipczak
Discusses values, ethics, and working styles that embrace generational differences and issues.

Podcasts

Code Switch: Race and Identity, Remixed
Discusses the overlap of race, socioeconomics, ethnicity, and culture, and how they play out in our lives and communities.

Focus on Ability
Interviews people with different abilities in the workplace.

Nevertheless
Focuses on women in tech and the ramifications when their suggestions aren't implemented.

Safe for Work
Interviews people about ageism at work.

The Secret Lives of Black Women
Interviews black women in high-profile roles in tech or tech-adjacent roles.

The Will to Change: Uncovering True Stories of Diversity and Inclusion
Tackles diversity in tech through the lens of women.

References

American Psychological Association. "Stress in America: Coping with Change." February 15, 2017. www.apa.org/news/press/releases /stress/2016/coping-with-change.pdf.

American Psychological Association. "Stress in America: The Impact of Discrimination." March 10, 2016. www.apa.org/news/press/releases /stress/2015/impact-of-discrimination.pdf.

Americans with Disabilities Act of 1990, as Amended, Pub. L. 110-325 (2008). Accessed November 19, 2019. www.ada.gov/pubs/adastatute08 .htm.

Anderson, Kathryn Freeman. "Diagnosing Discrimination: Stress from Perceived Racism and the Mental and Physical Health Effects." *Sociological Inquiry* 83, no. 1 (February 2013): 55–81. doi.org/10.1111 /j.1475-682X.2012.00433.x.

Blackburn, Sarah-Soonling. "What Is the Model Minority Myth?" *Teaching Tolerance*, March 21, 2019. www.tolerance.org/magazine /what-is-the-model-minority-myth.

Centers for Disease Control and Prevention. "Mental Health in the Workplace." Accessed November 21, 2019. www.cdc.gov/workplace healthpromotion/tools-resources/workplace-health/mental-health /index.html.

Civil Rights Act of 1964, Pub. L. 88-352, 78 Stat. 241 (1964). Accessed November 19, 2019. www.eeoc.gov/eeoc/history/35th/thelaw/civil _rights_act.html.

Civil Rights Amendments, H.R. 166, 94th Cong. (1975). www.congress .gov/bill/94th-congress/house-bill/166/all-info.

Condé Nast. "Code of Conduct." Last modified January 2018. www.condenast.com/code-of-conduct.

Crenshaw, Kimberlé. "Demarginalizing the Intersection of Race and Sex: A Black Feminist Critique of Antidiscrimination Doctrine, Feminist Theory and Antiracist Politics." *University of Chicago Legal Forum* 1989, article 8. chicagounbound.uchicago.edu/uclf/vol1989/iss1/8.

Decker, Scott H., Cassia Spohn, and Natalie R. Ortiz. "Criminal Stigma, Race, Gender, and Employment: An Expanded Assessment of the Consequences of Imprisonment for Employment." Final report to the National Institute of Justice. (2014). http://thecrimereport.s3.amazonaws .com/2/fb/e/2362/criminal_stigma_race_crime_and_unemployment.pdf.

Elias, Paul, "Judge: Abercrombie Wrongly Fired Muslim for Hijab." *USA Today*, September 9, 2013. www.usatoday.com/story/money /business/2013/09/09/judge-abercrombie-fitch-wrongly-fired-muslim -for-hibjab/2790721/.

Equal Pay Act of 1963, 29 U.S.C. § 206(d). Accessed November 19, 2019. www.eeoc.gov/laws/statutes/epa.cfm.

Equal Pay Today. "Equal Pay Days 2019." Accessed November 22, 2019. www.equalpaytoday.org/equalpaydays.

Equality Act of 2019, H.R. 5, 116th Cong. (2019). www.congress.gov/bill /116th-congress/house-bill/5/text?r=10.

Fair Labor Standards Act of 1938, as Amended, 29 U.S.C. §§ 201 *et seq.* Accessed November 22, 2019. www.dol.gov/whd/regs/statutes/fairlabor standact.pdf.

Fowler, Susan. "Reflecting on One Very, Very Strange Year at Uber." *Susan Fowler* (blog). February 19, 2017. www.susanjfowler.com/blog /2017/2/19/reflecting-on-one-very-strange-year-at-uber.

Frye, Jocelyn. *The Missing Conversation about Work and Family: Unique Challenges Facing Women of Color.* Center for American Progress. October 2016. https://cdn.americanprogress.org/wp-content /uploads/2016/09/30124619/WorkAndFamily-WomenOfColor-Oct.pdf.

Goldstein, Dana. "How Higher Ed Contributes to Inequality." *CityLab,* April 9, 2014. www.citylab.com/equity/2014/04/how-higher-ed-contributes -inequality/8841/.

Harris, Adam. "White College Graduates Are Doing Great with Their Parents' Money." *The Atlantic,* July 20, 2018. www.theatlantic.com /education/archive/2018/07/black-white-wealth-gap-inheritance/565640/.

Hill, Anita. "How History Changed Anita Hill." Interview by Jessica Bennett. *The New York Times,* June 17, 2019. www.nytimes.com/2019 /06/17/us/anita-hill-women-power.html.

Lilly Ledbetter Fair Pay Act of 2009, Pub. L. No. 111-2, 123 Stat. 5 (2009). www.govinfo.gov/content/pkg/PLAW-111publ2/pdf/PLAW-111publ2.pdf.

McKinsey & Company and LeanIn.org. *Women in the Workplace 2018.* Accessed November 19, 2019. https://womenintheworkplace.com /Women_in_the_Workplace_2018.pdf.

Mihalcik, Carrie. "Google Pays $11M to Settle with Job Seekers Who Alleged Age Discrimination." *CNET.com.* July 23, 2019. www.cnet.com /news/google-pays-11m-to-settle-with-job-seekers-who-alleged-age -discrimination/.

National Conference of State Legislatures. "Same-Sex Marriage Laws." Last modified June 26, 2015. www.ncsl.org/research/human-services /same-sex-marriage-laws.aspx.

Nunn, Ryan, Jimmy O'Donnell, and Jay Shambaugh. *A Dozen Facts about Immigration.* Brookings Institute. October 9, 2018. www.brookings.edu /research/a-dozen-facts-about-immigration/.

Pao, Ellen. "This Is How Sexism Works in Silicon Valley." *The Cut* (blog). *New York,* August 21, 2017. www.thecut.com/2017/08/ellen-pao -silicon-valley-sexism-reset-excerpt.html.

Pew Research Center. "Racial, Gender Wage Gaps Persist in U.S. Despite Some Progress." July 1, 2016. www.pewresearch.org/fact-tank/2016/07 /01/racial-gender-wage-gaps-persist-in-u-s-despite-some-progress/.

Rehabilitation Act of 1973, Pub. L. 92-112 (1973). Accessed November 19, 2019. www.eeoc.gov/eeoc/history/35th/thelaw/rehab_act-1973.html.

Rueb, Emily S. "JPMorgan Chase Stops Funding Private Prison Companies, and Immigration Acitivists Applaud." *New York Times*, March 6, 2019. www.nytimes.com/2019/03/06/business/jp-morgan-prisons.html.

Smedley, Brian D. "The Lived Experience of Race and Its Health Consequences." *American Journal of Public Health* 102, no. 5 (May 2012): 933–35. doi.org/10.2105/AJPH.2011.300643.

Teare, Gené, and Ned Desmond. "The First Comprehensive Study on Women in Venture Capital and Their Impact on Female Founders." *Tech Crunch*, April 19, 2016. https://techcrunch.com/2016/04/19/the-first-comprehensive-study-on-women-in-venture-capital/.

Telford, Taylor, and Renae Merle. "Bank of America Cuts Business Ties with Detention Centers, Private Prisons." *Washington Post*, June 27, 2019. www.washingtonpost.com/business/2019/06/27/bank-america-cuts-business-ties-with-detention-centers-private-prisons/.

U.S. Bureau of Labor Statistics. "Labor Force Characteristics by Race and Ethnicity, 2017." (August 2018). www.bls.gov/opub/reports/race-and-ethnicity/2017/home.htm.

U.S. Constitution, amendments XI–XXVII. Accessed November 12, 2019. www.archives.gov/founding-docs/amendments-11-27.

U.S. Constitution, the Bill of Rights. Accessed November 12, 2019. www.archives.gov/founding-docs/bill-of-rights.

U.S. Equal Employment Opportunity Commission. "What You Should Know about the EEOC and Religious and National Origin Discrimination Involving the Muslim, Sikh, Arab, Middle Eastern and South Asian Communities." Accessed November 19, 2019. www.eeoc.gov/eeoc/newsroom/wysk/religion_national_origin_9-11.cfm.

Index

Acknowledgments

I've always loved writing from the moment I learned how, as an outlet, as an expression of creativity, and a means to impart wisdom to others. Imagine my surprise and honor at being asked to write a book, by a tech-enabled publisher, on diversity—it was literally my dream!

To have this book debut during my 40th rotation around the sun is all I could have hoped for. I get to check off a bucket-list item during a year I want to spend in gratitude and reflection.

A number of people cheered me on, listened to me bemoan the process, and even let me interview them! I am eternally grateful for my family (Jaime, Gabriel, and Adrienne) and friends (especially Shanyn, Cydney, and Tamika) putting up with me interviewing people during late nights, early mornings, weekends, and vacations—and even skipping vacations (sorry, Shanyn!)—and whining to all of them.

I owe the same debt of gratitude to all of the wonderful people in this book who shared their personal stories, when it could've been easier to just say no, not reveal their hardships, or even their names. I cannot thank these 25 remarkable individuals enough for giving of their time, talents, and tales.

My editor, Crystal Nero, was a true gem. She worked with me against work deadlines, conferences, kid illnesses, injuries, emergency room visits, and consulting work to give me a schedule that ended up being doable, if not often appearing reasonable (lol). She acted not just as taskmaster but as cheerleader and knew when to straddle that line, or do both, effortlessly.

Lastly, thank you to my mother and grandmother, who taught me not only the power of reading but the power of my own voice, in whatever medium I choose to use it. They were lifelong teachers and told me I'd be one. I rejected that notion in the third grade. However, once I started writing articles and speaking, my mother told me, softly, one day, "You are a teacher; you just didn't know it, and it just doesn't look how you expected." I appreciate being taught and reassured there is power in our stories, and in my storytelling. So, thank you to Bettye and Linda for being great role models of how to teach and be effective, and I only hope to impart that same wisdom, love of learning, sense of empowerment, and confidence to Gabriel and Adrienne. I love you.

About the Author

Bärí A. Williams, Esq., is a legal and operations tech executive, start-up advisor in the tech industry, and author who has been published in the *New York Times*, *WIRED*, *Fortune*, and *Fast Company*. She is the former head of business operations management for North America at StubHub.

Prior to StubHub, Bärí was lead counsel at Facebook for teams that built drones and supported the supply chain. She also successfully created Facebook's Supplier Diversity Program, launched in October 2016.

Printed in the USA
CPSIA information can be obtained
at www.ICGtesting.com
LVHW060211031223
765101LV00004B/38